Unfiltered

No Shame, No Regrets, Just Me.

Unfiltered

No Shame, No Regrets, Just Me.

BY

LILY COLLINS

HARPER
An Imprint of HarperCollinsPublishers

Unfiltered: No Shame, No Regrets, Just Me.

Text copyright © 2017 by Secondary Shadow Inc.

ISBN 978-0-06-247302-8

Typography by Alison Klapthor
18 19 20 21 22   PC/LSCH   10 9 8 7 6 5 4 3 2 1
❖
First paperback edition, 2018

For all those who have ever felt alone . . .

To the incredibly inspiring young women around the world
whom I've had the pleasure of meeting in person or on
social media: Thank you for your constant support, passion,
encouragement, and love. Your bravery to bare your souls and
share your stories has inspired me to do the same.

Love Always
and
Forever

TABLE OF CONTENTS

Unfiltered

No Shame, No Regrets, Just Me.

Standing out in a crowd is much more rewarding than blending in.

1

THE QUIRKY THINGS THAT MAKE YOU DIFFERENT ARE WHAT MAKE YOU BEAUTIFUL

I used to be extremely insecure about my eyebrows. They've always had a mind of their own. When I moved to LA in elementary school, thin brows were the "in" thing. But since I was only six at the time, I wasn't paying attention to the media or the fashion world, nor did I feel the desire to change according to trends. I just knew I looked different. Once I hit twelve, though, and my preteen insecurities developed, I became *very* aware of my brows. They were all I could see when I looked in the mirror. They were so big and bushy and took up half my face. Kids started to make mean comments about them and it really got to me. Desperate for the insults to stop, I decided to take matters into my own hands.

One night before my mom and I were going out for dinner, I took a pair of tweezers and went to town on my brows. After what felt like forever, I stood back and admired myself in the mirror. I thought I'd done an amazing job: they each had a nice arch and looked even and equally separated. I was super proud! My mom and I drove to the restaurant and got a table without mentioning my plucking job. I was so nervous to know what she thought, I'd avoided her eyes the whole car ride. Well, that was no longer possible once we were across from each other at the table. My mom just sat there, staring at me, and asked what I'd done to my face. At first she genuinely couldn't figure out what was different, until it finally clicked. I said *I* thought my eyebrows looked great. She said she did not. She informed me I'd plucked half of them off and now they were two lines straight across my forehead. I refused to believe her, getting defensive and trying to justify why I'd done it. Then I went to the bathroom and stared long and hard at myself. Ugh, she was right. They really did look a hot mess. I couldn't believe it. I was instantly regretful and sulked back to the table. My mom tried to make me feel better, but then added that they might never grow back, which did NOT help. I was not only annoyed with myself but also terrified that my once-luscious (though somewhat unwieldy) brows were forever thinned out and I'd always look like a fool.

Well, BrowGate definitely taught me an important lesson. I'd let other kids' negative comments affect me, and then I'd let my insecurities lead me to alter my appearance and make a big mistake. Which was exactly why my mom was upset. She wanted me to recognize that I'd tried to change one of my features to fit in. I hadn't seen my thick, bushy brows as beautiful; I'd seen them only as something that made me different. So she taught me the mantra "The quirky things that make you different are what make you beautiful." Different shouldn't be considered a bad thing. Different *is* beautiful!

Luckily, my brows did grow back . . . albeit after quite some time. And I never went crazy on them again. It took me a while to fully embrace how prominent and unique they are, but once I did, I never went back! While I am still faced with negative comments online every day—people saying that I should shave or wax them off, that I'm too hairy—I just laugh and roll my eyes. I've grown so attached to my brows (and they to me) over the years. They've become my signature feature! Aside from the internet trolls, I get compliments on them all the time. I've even been asked by people if they could touch them. It's like they're rubbing the stomach of a Buddha statue for good luck! Despite being slightly confused by all this fuss, I'm super flattered. My brows have become a characteristic that defines *me*, rather than a characteristic that defines how I feel. They're part of who I am, and that's exactly the point: they're part of what makes me *me*. A trademark. There's only one of each of us in this world, so all those quirks that define us are special things that should be embraced, never pushed away.

Quirky isn't only about the physical characteristics we're born with. It can also be about our personality traits. Growing up, I was fascinated by what made people tick and loved finding any excuse to socialize with strangers. I genuinely wanted to meet new people from all walks of life and get to know them, and I craved the gratification that came from making others and, by extension, myself happy. I used to go up to people on the street and compliment them, telling a lady I liked her shoes, hair, dress, you name it, or even telling a guy he was handsome. My friends found it so weird, and they definitely didn't understand where I got the guts to do it—being super extroverted wasn't their style. Like the time I was nine and waiting on line at an amusement park with my mom and, with her approval, I approached this intriguing-looking thirtysomething guy in line in front of us. I told him I thought he was cute. I then asked him to sit next to me on the roller coaster because I was scared and knew his cuteness would distract me. As you might expect, he was thrown at first but, eventually, ended up caving. See! I was always weirdly brave around strangers, compelled to interact with them and befriend them even at the risk of embarrassing myself. I still remember going up to a heavily tattooed guy on a Harley-Davidson in Venice Beach when I was six and telling him in my sweet, inno-cent British accent that his tattoos were very pretty. Now, I'm sure that wasn't what he was expecting, nor what he wanted to hear in front of his fellow bikers, but I bet it made him smile on the inside. And I think that's why I did it. Not because I expected anything in return, but because I was never afraid to put myself out there in order to make someone else feel better. Which is very similar to what I often do as an actor: I help bring to life stories that I hope will make people feel comforted or happy. And there's nothing wrong with wanting to spread a little happiness. It's beautiful.

I WAS ALWAYS TELLING STORIES TO WHOEVER WOULD LISTEN—
GNOMES INCLUDED. I DIDN'T DISCRIMINATE.

This sort of quirky free-spiritedness didn't stop there. Ever since I was little, I've sought out the company of people much older than me. As a kid I didn't care that a grown-up and I had seemingly little in common, because once we got chatting, we had lots to say. Sometimes I even had more to talk about with them than with kids my age. Adults would ask me all kinds of questions about my generation and what certain words meant or what was cool. And I found them world-wise and hilarious. In fact, I made sure to include my friends' moms in conversations, while my friends would have rather ignored them. Being so close with my own mom, I loved hearing her friends' stories and found their conversations really interesting. Maybe it was considered odd that I was socializing with people triple my age, but I genuinely didn't think twice about it. And the wisdom they imparted to me was really valuable. Being open and nonjudgmental is an incredible thing. After all, it's how we'd want others to be toward us.

So who cares if some people didn't understand my outgoing nature or my love of socializing! Who cares if I was often the youngest person in the room! I've realized that whenever I feel self-conscious about any of my quirks, it's because I assume people are judging me. That's where the danger lies. You damage your own self-image when you compare yourself to others and to what you see in the media. And even though I'm in those magazines, movies, and shows, for a long time, I still did it, too. But once I accepted myself as I am, quirks included, it didn't matter how others viewed me because *I* liked what I saw. When people point out your differences as negative, it's only because they're insecure themselves. It can be extremely hard not to take personally, but the second we allow that to happen, we give power and truth to their words.

I may not have always behaved—hell, I may not always behave now—in a way that was expected, but how boring would it be if we all followed the same rules and did what was expected? Yeah, pretty damn boring. So let's proudly share our quirks. Be you and embrace your differences as things that make you unique and special. "Different" shouldn't be considered confusing, negative, or something that divides us. It should be a quality we applaud and admire within ourselves and others. Whenever

I sense any self-doubt creeping in to make me feel like an alien, I repeat my mom's mantra to myself—"The quirky things that make you different are what make you beautiful"—and I remember that standing out in a crowd is much more rewarding than blending in.

I will never need
anyone to complete me.
I am enough on my own.

"WHEN SOMEONE SHOWS YOU WHO
THEY ARE, BELIEVE THEM"

've found that some people are really great at hiding. Pretending.
Lying. Lying about what they feel, what they believe, and
about who they are entirely. Their lies are habitual, practically
subconscious, and exceptionally damaging. And sometimes I
didn't realize I'd fallen into them, and those are the times when
I became the most entangled, most lost, and most hurt.

I like to think I'm a pretty good judge of character. Growing
up in LA—a place deeply fascinated by celebrity—I got really
good at recognizing the ulterior motives of kids who wanted to
be my friends. I could see right through their insincerity. Despite
developing those observational skills early on, years later I still

found myself in a romantic relationship filled with deceit, infatuation, codependency, and some pretty dark shit. However hard it is to admit, I know now that I fell for his persona, the one he desperately wanted everyone to believe. Whenever anyone with a position of any kind of power (real or imagined) chooses you over everyone else, it's natural to get caught up in that. In my situation, there were so many intriguing aspects to who he was and what it would be like to be together, I couldn't help wanting to explore them. But all of my assumptions were based on what I *thought* I knew, not on reality.

I found myself trapped, hiding from the harsh reality that I'd lost myself by pretending to be what he wanted. It's awful when your relationship doesn't feel right but, instead of trusting your instincts, you decide there's something wrong with you and it would be easier to blame yourself: *Everything is fine. He's fine. I'm fine. He's right. I'm wrong. I made a mistake. It's my fault.*

The pain wasn't obvious to me at first. I was completely caught up in him, in us, in the honeymoon-phase bliss. I was focused on making sure that I was perfect for him, that I was happy all the time, that I never gave him any reason to leave. But the more I silenced my voice with this guy, the more isolated I became. I didn't recognize myself drifting further and further away from my friends. They tried so many times to open my eyes to what was happening and to help me, but I couldn't hear them.

I didn't want to believe that I was being tricked into thinking my boyfriend was someone he wasn't.

Our love story progressed at lightning speed, with neither of us playing coy about how we felt. The beginning was filled with anticipation and excited butterflies. For a while it was fun keeping things private, just between us. We texted and called each other constantly. We seemed much like any other young couple madly in love.

The arguments started a couple months later. I began to see a very different side of him: curtness, a belittling tone, verbal reprimands. We worked through these issues daily, and he would send me letters expressing intense and all-consuming love to make up for his behavior. He once wrote that he didn't know what he'd do without me and that it scared him. What the hell is a girl supposed to do when she reads that? Of course there was a sense of security knowing that I was the one he needed, that there was something about me that made him feel safe and loved. But immense uneasiness also came with it. I felt hypocritical because, on one hand, I *did* want all this attention from him. Yet when he came on so strong, I felt scared and claustrophobic and out of control. Still, I loved him and couldn't see myself without him, so I ignored the red flags and passed them off as things that would fix themselves.

Things continued to escalate and I no longer felt the "safety" that had helped me justify putting up with his abuse. His old habits trumped any security his love letters provided and he was back to telling me what I could and couldn't do, should and shouldn't wear—everything I did was "inappropriate," a word that still haunts me to this day. He yelled at me, calling me horrible things like dumb, blind, stupid, selfish, and a whore. I was made to feel unworthy, less than, and, frankly, like a piece of shit. He told me to "suck cock" one night on the phone and then he hung up after saying there was no point even talking to me.

He silenced any voice I thought I had, both inwardly and outwardly. My opinions were disregarded, my feelings dismissed, and my body weakened. I had panic attacks where my heart beat out of my chest as I sobbed and hyperventilated on the floor. I was so stressed that I developed rashes and acne. I found myself second-guessing every thought I had and every choice I made. Whenever I spent time with him, I was basically hidden away in his house with the blinds drawn. Even though my close friends and family knew we were together, it still felt like we were meant to be kept a secret. Long gone were the days of that harmless fun, that sacred intimacy. It wasn't exciting to sneak around, living in constant anxiety of being "discovered." I wasn't looking for a public declaration of love. Simple hand-holding would have sufficed.

I had completely isolated myself, made my world so small.

He became my world and made me feel like my only place was with him. He discouraged me from seeing certain people, mostly other guys I'd been friends with for years. Any social life that didn't involve him or his friends was unacceptable. Even my relationship with my own mom, which means the world to me, was challenged. I became a one-woman island, but not the strong and independent kind. I was the definition of codependent. And worst of all: I became so scared that if I left him, I would have nothing. Be nothing.

I'll never forget the moment when the verbal threats escalated and signs of physical violence started to show. His temper had flared up and he was being very verbally aggressive again, and in the middle of an argument his hand reached out and closed around my neck. Part of me feels strange even calling it choking because I can't imagine this person doing such a thing, yet it still felt extremely threatening. It shocked me to the core and was what made *me* finally take notice. People close to me had already voiced their concerns about his demeanor; they felt we were ill-suited for each other. But their concerns had been based solely on what they'd seen on the surface, never on what was happening behind closed doors that only the two of us knew. The whole incident left me scared and confused. I wanted to reach out for help from those who had already spoken up, but didn't want to expose what had really been going on or get him in trouble. I also didn't want them to think less of me for being in this situation.

My mom was the one who finally encouraged me to speak with a very dear friend who had been in this same kind of relationship years before. We sat for a couple of hours and talked about our shared experiences, and at the end he looked at me so powerfully and said: "When someone shows you who they are, believe them." With that simple statement—originally coined by Maya Angelou—it all clicked.

My boyfriend was a yeller, a name-caller, a belittler, a loose cannon. He had consistently shown me who he was, and I was still trying to convince myself that I could change him. I thought I could make him less angry, less demanding, less abusive by being a better girlfriend. But that wasn't going to change anything. Sure, maybe it would get easier for a day, a week, even a month. But ultimately if he was capable of making me feel less than, making me doubt myself, my heart, my gut, and my intellect—then he wasn't the person I should be with.

Not long after this discussion, I broke things off and we didn't speak for a while. However—and I know many of you will be in absolute shock when I say this—he convinced me, after we spent that time apart, that we should talk it all through face-to-face. We did just that and, during our discussion, we discovered we'd both done our own self-reflection to better understand how to move forward. So we decided to try again. I planned to speak up more, and he'd be more attentive and understanding.

I was excited to apply these new promises and felt mature knowing we'd been so open and honest with each other about how to move forward. This was a step in the right direction. Or so I thought.

Things seemed to hold firm because we were all lovey-dovey again. He constantly told me how much he loved me, banishing any doubt that I was worthy of his affection, and he stressed how no one would ever love me like he did. I felt important and irreplaceable. Yes, there were hiccups here and there, but sometimes it was as if the earlier months had melted away and he was a different person altogether. Those moments of hope, of a brighter future ahead, were what kept me motivated to keep trying.

But despite our best efforts, eventually old habits reared their ugly heads and things went back to the way they used to be. There came a point when being wooed with gifts and words of affirmation and love wasn't enough. Nothing he said or did felt genuine anymore, and I started to see his threats as empty.

It was time for another intervention, this time on the phone with my mom and with friends. They begged me to value myself again and to see a future where these problems no longer existed. They reminded me of who I was and inspired an inner strength that had been weakened for so long. I listened wholeheartedly and finally heard them. Within minutes of hanging up the phone, I ended the relationship for good—a relationship I will always look back on as the one where I disappeared.

So why did I put up with it? Why did I stay? Because, at the end of the day, he showed me love—or what I thought was love. He acted as if his cruelty had never happened, as if I'd blown everything out of proportion. Or he'd simply apologize over and over again. He'd wear me down each time it happened, so it started to feel normal and, in a way, expected. I never knew what version of him I was going to get, so I lived in a constant state of fear and uncertainty. But the uncertainty became normal and, furthermore, comfortable. As sick as it may sound, during the good times, I started believing that no one would love me as strongly as him or treat me as well. This, I've come to learn, is what psychological manipulation looks like at its finest.

He and I loved each other. I thought I needed him to complete me, to survive, because that's what he wanted me to believe. I was afraid to say good-bye; afraid he'd still be able to control me even after we weren't together—control my decisions and my future relationships. But I will never need anyone to complete me. I am enough on my own. Unfortunately, at that point, I hadn't yet learned that lesson.

My gut told me many times that the situation wasn't right. But I kept convincing myself that it was *me* who needed to work harder at the relationship so that he wouldn't doubt me, be angry with me, or tell me off. I now see that my boyfriend was dealing with his own identity crisis and insecurities, all of which he projected onto me. By controlling *me*, he could forget about the fact that he couldn't control the thoughts in his own head. He wasn't happy within himself so he tried to make me feel the same. But I was so deep in the situation, desperately wishing to be accepted and desired by this person, that I didn't have the courage to stand up. It wasn't until I reached my limit, when my body felt like it was shutting down, that I finally recognized I needed to end it.

Knowing what I know now about what it feels like to be truly adored, loved, and respected—not only by someone else but also by myself—I find it a mystery how I stayed trapped by these insecurities for so long. Thinking back on it, I now realize: I didn't value myself enough. I didn't have faith that I was enough as I was. I was too weak to know that it's okay to disagree with someone I'm in a romantic relationship with. It's okay to stand up for myself and assert my opinions. Expressing myself in any relationship should never be considered complaining. I don't need to be afraid that saying one thing will cause him to leave. And, honestly, if that's the case and he does, why would I want to be with him anyway?

I don't regret any of the decisions I've made or the people I've chosen to be with, as I truly do believe everything happens for a reason. Sometimes we need to experience what we don't like in order to know what we do like. We need to be with the wrong person to recognize who the right one is, how he should treat us, and what kind of respect we deserve. This specific boyfriend, and a few that followed, taught me more about myself than I ever anticipated.

Emotional abuse is nothing to be taken lightly. It's an incredibly dangerous and disgusting thing that is far more common than I thought. For me, the hardest part about being in a relationship like that was how I never saw the light when I was so deeply in the dark. I was so enamored of him and blinded by the fact that he had chosen me out of everyone else, that I felt I had to be exactly the way he liked or else he'd leave me.

My friend's mantra, "When someone shows you who they are, believe them," continues to ring loudly in my ears and has changed my life. The more I chant it, the more I'm reminded of how easy it is to be fooled, to be tricked, to be lied to. Even though it took me a relationship relapse for the advice to really resonate, I have since fully digested it. And the stronger I get, the easier it becomes to take myself out of those kinds of situations and end them before I'm in too deep again. Because I've learned that this kind of behavior is not singular to romance. It exists in all facets of life. The feelings I felt, the abuse and manipulation I endured, can be experienced in my interactions with people

I love, those I work with, even random humans I meet on the street. The world is made up of all kinds of people and I'm not always going to get along with everyone. As long as I know that I have the choice in how I interact with them and to what degree I allow them to affect me, they can't dampen my spirit or turn off my light. No relationship is greater than the one I have with myself. I just need to trust my gut, follow my instincts, and when someone shows me who they are, believe them.

You deserve happiness.
You deserve to be loved
just as you love others.
You deserve everything.

WE ACCEPT THE LOVE WE THINK WE DESERVE

A letter to remind us all that we deserve to be treated with kindness and respect. And that we should never settle for anything less than what we deserve, no matter how we've been treated in the past. This can be torn out and folded in your wallet, pinned up on your wall or mirror, or simply read once and then put away for a rainy day.

A note to self:

I know I find it really difficult to love me sometimes, but I vow to always try my best. There are days when I feel like

I'm not good enough, strong enough, just simply not enough.
Those days are some of the hardest. They test the weakest
parts of me and trigger doubt, distress, and pain. But, more
importantly, they are the days that build up my inner strength
and define my true sense of self. No matter what I've endured
in the past, what I've put myself through, or what others have
done to me—I have the ability and the will to move forward.
I will not give up. I will not undervalue or underestimate my
capabilities. I can't look to someone else to be my everything
or rely on them to make me feel whole. I am whole just as I
am. I am defined, not by my life experiences, but by how I let
them affect me and how I handle myself in each situation. Just
because someone treats me badly doesn't mean that I am a bad
person or unworthy. It definitely doesn't mean I must treat
myself the same way. I know I've felt abandoned, ashamed,
and let down. I know I've been hurt. I also know I've hurt
myself to draw my attention away from the pain inflicted on
me by others. But that doesn't help anything. It doesn't change
the other person and it certainly doesn't change what happened.
I need to open my eyes and let the light in. I know the darkness
can become all too comfortable and normal. I begin to expect
it. But it doesn't have to be so. And, at the same time, I must
acknowledge that the darkness is important because I can't
know what the light feels like without it. It isn't all bad. When

someone else casts their darkness on me, I can use it to learn and to grow. I shouldn't dwell on the things they said to me or the way they made me feel. Those words were not true. They were not kind. And I deserve to be spoken to only with kindness. My worth is not defined by their actions because their actions are not a reflection of my worth. Those actions say much more about who they are than who I am. When I love, I love hard. And I won't let someone trample over my heart. I won't convince myself that they were, and still are, the only person who will ever love me. That's not love. That's not how love is supposed to feel. But there is someone out there who will show me what real, honest love is. They will respect and accept me for me and won't make me feel less than. In order to find that person and truly let them in, first I must believe in myself and know my own value. It's not selfish to want these things nor is it selfish to think them. I deserve happiness. I deserve to be loved just as I love others. I deserve everything. I must forgive myself for being in some of the situations I've been in. For staying. For putting up with less than I deserve. There is no shame in what I went through. Forgiving myself is just as important as forgiving others. But now I know. Now I know I deserve to be the happiest, most fulfilled version of myself that I can possibly be. And I promise to use my experiences to continue to grow, heal, and expand my life. It starts with me.

In order to accept the love I deserve from someone else, I must truly believe that I am worthy of it. And I am. And I'll never let anyone tell me differently.

I value myself. I respect myself. I appreciate myself. I accept myself. I love myself. Always and forever.

Me xo

Love will find you again.
And you can never, ever
change yourself for
anyone or change yourself
to fix the relationship.
So if it isn't healthy,
say good-bye.

4

GREAT DISAPPEARING ACTS

'm the first to admit that I'm completely obsessed with magic. I have always loved and will always love anything involving the supernatural—from movies to live performances, from Harry Potter to *The Sixth Sense*. I'm fascinated by the unexplainable and by how magicians pull off their magic tricks. But ever since I started dating, I've become familiar with a whole new type of trick, one mastered by tons of guys out there. It's something I like to call The Great Disappearing Act. It doesn't require costumes or tools, riddles or rhymes—just two people seemingly getting along and entering into some form of a relationship . . . until the moment one of them just, POOF!, disappears. This trick also goes by the name of ghosting, if that's more familiar to you.

Of all the magic tricks I've tried to understand over the years, this one has proved to be the most difficult. At this point you'd think I'd be able to anticipate it, but I never do. That's the worst part: we rarely see it coming, and then we're left doubting, even blaming ourselves for the *other person's* lack of maturity.

My first experience with being ghosted was when I had been seeing someone for a while and all of a sudden he literally just stopped communicating with me. One day we were hanging out; the next he went MIA. Naturally I was confused and assumed I'd done something wrong. I left it alone, not wanting to seem needy or anxious. A couple weeks went by without seeing him or hearing a word, and then out of the blue we ran into each other. I didn't want to bring it up or cause a scene, but I couldn't say nothing! So I very coolly confronted him and asked what had happened, since everything had seemed perfectly fine leading up to his disappearance. He brushed it off, saying he'd contact me later that week so he could explain everything—he said he owed it to me. *Well*. I never heard from him!

Cut to two years later. I ran into the same guy and he asks me to hang out *again*. Now, I'm well aware of that saying "Fool me once, shame on you; fool me twice, shame on me." But I also like to see the best in people and give them the benefit of the doubt. So when he told me he had matured and was super sorry about the way he'd handled things, I believed him. I really did think he'd changed! We slowly started seeing each other casually. I was way more vocal this time, unafraid to voice my opinions and feelings. And it was making a huge difference. One night he blew me off, and then texted suggesting we hang out hours after our planned date. I said it was too late at that point and I wasn't cool with the way he'd handled the situation. Within an hour he showed up at my door with flowers to apologize. So I assumed things were headed in a positive direction! That is . . . until I found out he was also texting a girlfriend of mine about hanging out. *Not. Cool. Again.* I confronted him. He said she was just a friend. She showed me the messages: you don't text that kind of thing to someone who's just a friend. I might have accepted that excuse the first time around, but the second time it happened, I had really had enough. He promised he would call the next day to figure out a time to come over and chat. He owed it to me AGAIN. Well, to this day, I still haven't heard anything. So I guess you could call that getting ghosted by the same guy twice. Feel free to think about *that* the next time you're feeling bummed out about a boy!

My second ghosting experience was after a more serious relationship with someone. I'd learned a great deal about myself during my time with him, and I'd reached a point where I needed to express some very real concerns about possible addictions he was battling. I did so in a way that was sensitive, yet strong, and very conversational. I was super proud of myself for having the guts to voice all of it and for knowing myself well enough to recognize my own limits! After hearing me out, he suggested we both take some time to think things through and then talk. I respected that he needed to digest what I'd said. And I needed to figure out where we could go from there.

But I guess I'll never know 'cause I never heard back! And it really, really sucked that time. As months passed and my voice mails and texts went unanswered, I remained confused and utterly heartbroken. But my eyes were certainly opened. Even though I'll always have love for that guy and will support him through whatever he needs, I had to let it go. Let *him* go. Because if he couldn't admit his feelings, step up to the plate, and meet me in the middle to discuss things—that's all I needed to know.

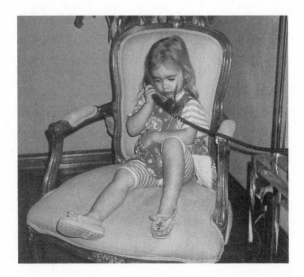

UMMM, HELLOOOO? I SHOULD HAVE KNOWN BACK THEN
THAT HIS SILENCE WAS A SIGN. . . .

A more recent ghosting adventure was with someone who gave me zero indication that he was anything other than a complete gentleman. We spent a few weeks hanging out pretty regularly doing fun and adventurous things and then, the morning after an incredible date, I received The Text. I understood and appreciated that he didn't want a serious relationship (neither did I, by the way), but I also had some things to say. And I wanted to say them in person rather than over text. DO YOU THINK I GOT THAT CHANCE? Hell no! I heard not a word. He got to say exactly what he wanted to, and then completely peaced out and disappeared. How unfair is that? What I felt, and what I needed to say, were completely disregarded and ignored. I was left feeling hurt, disappointed, and disrespected yet again. And I'd had *enough*. Luckily, I had the opportunity weeks later to call him out on it at a party and I took it, guns blazing. With a smile I very casually asked what had happened and he replied, "With what?" Um . . . WITH US, HELLO? I gave him a knowing look and repeated the question and he said it wasn't the time and walked away. Well, I wasn't about to let that be how it ended, so I went back up to him and said I wasn't trying to make anything awkward, just address the obvious. He started with the excuses—but stopped himself and asked if we could get together so he could properly explain it all. He wanted me to understand, thought I deserved to understand (which I did). Turns out he was all talk and no action! Let's just say I gave up on waiting. But, honestly, I felt so much better for at least having had my day in court and having the balls to address it how I did. I can't help that he was a coward.

If you'll notice, there's a definite pattern here: the second I called all these guys on their shit or stood up for myself and expressed my feelings, they fled. It's like they couldn't handle being confronted and, instead of being mature and having a rational conversation, they defaulted to silence. Well, their silence spoke volumes! And I realized those aren't the kinds of guys I want to be in relationships with. Even so, I started to believe I had to protect myself going forward. The more this kind of thing happened, the more sensitive I became and the more self-doubt I had. Because when I considered that the common denominator in all these situations was me, I automatically assumed that *I* was the problem. But let's be clear: you are never the problem in this kind of situation—they are. I promise.

Besides flat-out disappearing, there's also this phenomenon I like to call emotional ghosting, which is when someone is physically present but not emotionally connected to you. Sometimes it can be worse than classic ghosting. They may literally see us, but they're not seeing what we're saying or meaning. I guess you could call it selective hearing, too, which I'm sure we've all suffered through. With this one guy I dated, I'd say something to him and although he'd respond, he never actually addressed what I'd brought up. His evasive and vague answers were just enough to hold a conversation without actually engaging in it. His ignoring me was either intentional or the result of him constantly being on his cell phone. Also not cool. I'M RIGHT HERE! Or that time I was really concerned about an ex-boyfriend who was in recovery. After witnessing him struggle with addiction in the past, my female intuition kicked in and sensed that he was still battling some of his demons. When I tried time and time again to express my worries to him, it felt to me like he was deflecting. Though he was listening to my words from the other end of the phone or even sitting right in front of my face, he wasn't *hearing* me. He wasn't allowing me to connect or have a real conversation. It was as if I was physically reaching out to him, and when I went to grab his hand, mine went straight through his body like a ghost's.

ONE DAY IT'LL HAPPEN.
JUST HOPING I DON'T GET GHOSTED AT THE ALTAR. . . .

For quite a long time, in romantic relationships I always found myself staying quiet, either out of choice or because an ex insisted I be that way. But the older I got and the more I spoke up for myself, the more the guys literally started disappearing! I'd gather the courage and feel confident enough to be real, and then they'd vanish. It's hard to admit, but that chain of events sometimes taints my ability to move on and get back out there. A fear of the same thing happening creeps in. But you can't ever lose hope! Love will find you again. And you can never, ever change yourself for anyone or change yourself to fix the relationship. So if it isn't healthy, say good-bye. Staying true to who you are is all that matters, and if that true you is someone like me who wants to use her voice and face things head-on, then eventually the right person will come along who respects that confrontation and finds it empowering, attractive, and sexy.

There is a greater happiness to be attained: the happiness of enjoying myself to the fullest during the one life I have and accepting myself for who I am.

MY BATTLE FOR PERFECTION

Food is something we all need to survive—that fact is the same for everyone. But it's our *relationships* with food that define our differences.

I never had a problem eating whatever I wanted while growing up in England or when I first moved to LA. Back then, I never questioned my cravings or thought twice about ordering dessert. I was a normal kid; I was growing, I was healthy. No one made me feel self-conscious or made me doubt how good I looked. This is why it's hard for me to understand how I fell into such a deep trap years later—a trap I have slowly but surely been digging my way out of ever since.

I have so many amazing memories from elementary school

that are associated with food: lunches, dinners, playdates, Halloween celebrations, sports games. But those positive associations tapered off once I turned sixteen. Not only did I start viewing myself differently physically, but I began limiting my happiness by controlling my eating habits. At the time, my dad was separating from my stepmom and I was in the middle of high school, juggling a heavy workload, a social life, a budding modeling career, as well as pursuing acting. I had so many balls in the air and my life felt out of my control. I couldn't handle the pain and confusion surrounding my dad's divorce, and I was having a hard time balancing being a teenager with pursuing two different grown-up careers—both of which I'd chosen myself, but which also focused heavily on how I looked.

As if high school weren't enough of a self-confidence roller coaster, all these extra pressures made things even worse. I had always been involved in sports, but in high school I stopped being part of a team and started exercising solo. If I didn't have a meeting or audition after school, I went straight to the gym for an hour and a half. On one hand, I associated working out with stress because I became extremely anxious if there was a day I couldn't exercise. On the other hand, the second I started sweating, I felt a sense of relaxation, calm, and control—control over my workout schedule, my daily routine, how much energy I used, what I ate, and how many calories I burned. All of which ultimately enabled me to control how I looked. Sad as it sounds, I reveled in this obsessive way of thinking. I started to look more like how I thought I needed to in front of the camera, while also numbing my feelings about everything else going on in my life. Exercise became a form of self-medication.

Despite countless hours at the gym, I also restricted what and how much I ate throughout the school day. I basically starved myself, only eating foods when I knew their calorie count. I very rarely deviated from my "menu." And when I had strong cravings, I chewed gum, sometimes going through multiple packs a day. And let me tell you: gum does not do your stomach any favors; it may taste good in the moment, but it is not a remedy for hunger. And so I became addicted to gum and coffee, depending on them so much that my friends joked they never saw me without them. When I got home from school, I'd have a small snack (which I'd inevitably burn off in the gym later). Then dinner was usually my mom's cooking, which I'd loved ever since I was little. However, now that I was restricting myself, certain things she used to make were no longer "allowed." I requested the same meals over and over because I knew how many calories they had. And if she deviated by making something unexpected, I would have a silent panic attack. If we went out to dinner, I would order minimally and only from certain sections of the menu. I became the most boring person to cook for and the most annoying person to go out with.

My mom and my friends didn't notice my problem at first

because it was such a slow process; it's not like I started losing weight immediately. Believe me, that would have been fabulous. If I could have snapped my fingers and melted away the pounds, I would have been the happiest girl alive. But as I did get thinner, more people started to notice. I was flattered by the stares and comments. I thought I looked amazing, and if anyone said anything negative, I assumed they were envious. I assumed everyone just wanted to be skinny like me. Losing weight and attaining my version of perfection became my focus. It was then that I really started my battle with anorexia. Gone was the joy I had once associated with food. Going out to dinner with friends scared me because I didn't know what I'd order or how I'd get through it without being caught.

Since I was little, I'd always needed to eat everything on my plate in order to mentally feel full, even if physically I'd had enough. So, once I had the disorder, I still had to keep doing that. If I had stopped, I would have felt miserably hungry and it would have looked suspicious to my friends and family. Which meant that whatever I ordered had to be super healthy and very plain. I couldn't do shared plates anymore or try a bunch of different things. Eating was no longer a fun social event, but instead a chore and a punishment. I was exhausted and antsy and bitchy all the time. I sure as hell wasn't much fun. But my plan was working! I was in control! I was skinny! And, at the time, that was what mattered to me.

My diet pill and laxative addiction also started when I was around sixteen and continued into my early twenties. A girl I knew was raving about these energy pills that boosted your metabolism and claimed to melt away fat. Her mom had given them to her, which at the time I thought was pretty cool, but now realize is incredibly sick. I knew *my* mom would never be okay with them, so I started secretly buying them at drugstores and hiding them all over my room. It wasn't until years later that my mom would eventually uncover my addiction by finding the left-over opened boxes and pill bottles in the back of my bathroom cupboards that I'd forgotten to throw away. Much as I wanted to believe that these pills were helping me, they made my heart beat faster than should be humanly possible and gave me the worst headaches. I remember a day at school when I'd taken a couple of them while waiting for class to start. I had to sit down because I wasn't seeing straight, and my head felt like it was about to explode. I couldn't concentrate and was super agitated. It became totally normal for me to go through these cycles of extreme highs and then the most exhausting lows for weeks at a time.

To make matters worse, I then began bingeing and purging. Bulimia was another way I thought I could gain control during an emotionally unstable time in my life. Sometimes I promised I'd stop punishing myself this way, but then I'd get these intense food cravings I had to satisfy with bingeing, which then meant I had to purge. I saw things as all or nothing. I completely forbade myself from even tasting certain foods, terrified I'd eat them in excess. But then I'd go to the supermarket late at night and load up on every type of junk food possible and return home to my bedroom and just eat and eat. I'd finish boxes of cookies, pints of ice cream, cupcakes, slices of cake, and then go into my bathroom and throw it all up. I started by using a toothbrush, then a hair chopstick, and finally graduated to my finger. It was a "successful" session if I could purge it all. But if there was ever a time I knew that not everything had come back up, I'd spiral into a panic. This usually happened if I'd eaten so quickly that I hadn't had time to drink anything. I'd be in tears on the floor, jamming my hand down my throat and trying desperately to gag and expel the remainder of what I had allowed myself to eat.

I hated myself for doing this. But I felt accomplished, too, because I had quenched the craving while not having to "suffer" the external consequences. I could eat all this sugar and fat but not *become* fat. The crazy thing is that I was doing way more damage to myself than I even knew. Between the starvation, the diet pills, the laxatives, and throwing up, I not only lost all my energy, but my body started to shut down. My hair and nails lost their shine and became brittle. My throat burned and my esophagus ached. My period stopped for a couple years and I was terrified I had ruined my chances of having kids. I was convinced that I had fucked myself up beyond repair, but refused to acknowledge this fear enough to go get checked out. The longer I put it off, the longer my denial could continue and the more "perfection" I could attain. I was afraid of getting fat. Of no longer having that "perfect" image. I knew that I had a major problem and that there was a better way to live my life. But I couldn't stop. And, even worse, I didn't want to.

There did, however, come a point when my school had to intervene and my guidance counselor told my mom and me that if I didn't get a doctor's note saying I was at a healthy enough weight and not medically in danger, I wouldn't be allowed back at school. On the way to my eventual appointment, I was so terrified that the low number on the scale would dictate my future, I stopped at Starbucks and downed a few pastries so that I weighed more. The panic didn't settle in until later when I got home and thought about how all those carbs and sugar were just sitting in my stomach and how it was too late to get rid of them. In the end, I'm sure because of my binge, I weighed just enough not to technically be in danger and I got the all-powerful doctor's note. I was able to continue denying my problem at school and pursue this secret path of self-destruction.

Another memory from around that time is from a trip to England when I was driving home with my mom and she spontaneously wanted to stop somewhere to visit. I freaked out. I had a mini panic attack because it wasn't on "the schedule." I had become so accustomed to measuring out and prepackaging my food and dictating what I ate, knowing how to sustain just enough energy to get through the day—so that when she suggested we deviate, I didn't know what to do. We stopped anyway, and I dealt with it, but I was in such an awful mood and my mom noticed. How could she not? I think this was one of the first moments I couldn't control my reactions anymore or hide them from my mom. They started to control my life so badly and kept bubbling to the surface—until I finally exploded.

During my time battling these disorders, I went through major weight fluctuations. There were periods when I was super tiny, the worst of it being in 2008 and then again in 2013. When I gained, I felt like I'd fallen off the wagon and would then steadily start using my methods to lose again. There was no real maintenance program for me. No moderation. It was all or nothing, black or white. At my worst, I felt like a young woman in a little kid's body. I felt unfeminine, without any sex drive. But I was so obsessed with and absorbed by the entire sickness that I even used to ask my little brothers when they were around three years old if they thought I looked fat. To this day, I can't believe I sunk that low.

One of the worst side effects of maintaining and feeding my

disorders was that I lied to my mom for years about it. It's not at all that she was oblivious! Up until this whole overwhelming ordeal started, I had told her everything and shared any and all insecurities. We were best friends, and to hide something as serious as this was a huge deal. I know it must have been extremely confusing to see her little girl, who had always been confident and secure, suddenly be plagued with self-doubt. I know seeing me wither away caused her immense fear and despair. And I know I caused her so much pain when she found out exactly what I had been putting myself through. She'd thought of me as someone who loved exercise and was a picky eater, not as someone who was unhealthily obsessed with working out and intensely controlled their eating habits. It wasn't until I admitted my bingeing and purging that she finally knew the full spectrum of pain I'd inflicted on myself. Not surprisingly, she took it personally, as if she hadn't paid enough attention. But really, I had done such a good job of lying and hiding it. Hiding my pain. Hiding my ways of dealing with it. And hiding myself.

But I refuse to do that now. I alienated myself from friends and family for far too long. I lied, kept secrets, and felt good about it. I took comfort in the pain I was causing myself, and I saw a beauty within the incredibly ugly things I was putting myself through. I wasted so much time worrying about what I looked like and how much I could control my appearance that I missed out on making some wonderful memories in high school and learning what it means to come into my own body naturally. For years I didn't know what my body was supposed to look like or how it was supposed to feel. I had to begin the journey of re-familiarizing myself with the physical signs before my period, as well as how my body reacts to certain foods—which I am still working on today. I had to learn moderation. One of the happiest, most comforting days I can remember was finally working up the courage to go to the gynecologist and get checked out and having her tell me I was okay and would, indeed, one day be able to have children. After all I had put my body through, I hadn't screwed myself up for good.

As silent as I once was about my food issues, going forward I vow to be vocal and open. I never want my kids worrying about it like I did. I never want them to face their concerns or insecurities alone. No one feels perfect all the time. It's natural to have days where you look in the mirror and want to alter what you see. But taking it out on your body and punishing yourself is not the answer. No good came from lying, and skinny was not what I actually wanted. I wanted to feel in control of my insanely busy life, and I wanted to feel happy and content within my own skin. As soon as I realized that hiding would never bring me closer to those goals, I allowed myself to accept help and acknowledge that something was wrong. I finally listened to my mom's and my friends' concerns and took them seriously. In our conversations, I started to value myself more and prioritize the things I was looking forward to in life over short-lived gratification. I decided to find a therapist to work through some things I could no longer do on my own. For someone who wants to be the one who others come to for help, this was a huge step. If it meant I needed to be open and willing to accept help, then I was going to embrace it with open arms and an open heart.

Healing is an ongoing process, and I will be working through my disorders for the rest of my life. But I know now that there is a greater happiness to be attained in this world: the happiness of enjoying myself to the fullest during the one life I have and accepting myself for who I am while I'm living it.

My mom has instilled in me a true appreciation for life, an acceptance of who I am, and a greater understanding of what it means to be a mother.

MY MOM: THE MYTH, THE LEGEND

My mom is a total badass rock star. Always has been, always will be. And I honestly don't know where I'd be without her. Not a day goes by that I don't realize how lucky I am to have the beautiful relationship we do. She's my best friend, inspiration, role model, confidante, and partner in crime. The Jill to my Lil! Yes, we totally get on each other's nerves and drive each other crazy from time to time (like any mother and daughter). . . . But all that aside, I'd be lost without her.

Through my mom's love of exploration, I've acquired such an appreciation for life and culture. Whatever I was studying in school—whether it was ancient Egyptian history, African elephants, or foreign countries like India and Japan—she took me to those places so we could share in new adventures together and see it all firsthand. She believed the best way to learn was to immerse ourselves in the cultures and experience them as locals do. We became a professional traveling duo, skilled in the art of minimalist packing and survival techniques.

In 1999, we rode the train from LA to Santa Fe, New Mexico, where we took ghost tours and explored the city and the San Miguel Chapel for a school project on US missions I was doing. Later that year, we learned how to ignore massive wall spiders looming over us in Africa, traveling the terrain in canoes and open-top Jeeps, spotting all kinds of beautiful animals, and riding a classic steam train through the wilderness. We celebrated the millennium in Ecuador and stood on both sides of the equator. In 2001, in the jungles of Belize we visited ruins, flew in very questionable tiny airplanes, and finally learned how to catch scorpions after several nights of finding them in our bedsheets.

We navigated our way through the train system in Japan in 2003 (despite not understanding a word of Japanese), prayed at ancient temples, and visited a famous fish market/auction at five a.m. In 2005, we visited the Taj Mahal and took a boat cruise in Kerala, India, seeing locals go about their daily lives along the banks of the river. Mom celebrated her fiftieth birthday in 2006, fulfilling a lifelong dream of seeing the Egyptian pyramids (which we accomplished from our hotel room and, later, by climbing into one), visiting King Tut's tomb, and riding camels in the desert. She even stood by and watched as I got übercool cornrows in Cancún—yes, I went through *that* phase.

MOM AND ME OUTSIDE AN ELEPHANT CAMP IN AFRICA.

THAT PHASE.

WHAT A WONDER! BFFS IN FRONT OF THE EGYPTIAN PYRAMIDS.

But when it comes to traveling with my mom, "adventure" isn't just about getting on a plane and flying far away. Life is about exploring your own backyard, too. Ever since I was in elementary school, she would take me and my friends to places most of their parents would never dare. I mean, what's so scary about Venice Beach? She brought us to musicals, magic shows, flea markets, circuses, concerts, and art fairs. She exposed us to people from all walks of life and encouraged us to step outside our comfort zones and experience the unknown. She may not have been like the other moms, but she was *my* mom: forever the coolest, most innovative woman I knew, who found solutions to problems and supported my creativity and individuality.

Mom was always around to help me make pivotal life decisions, too. Never pushy, just there to listen and support and offer her two cents. When I was applying to high schools, I fell in love with Harvard-Westlake in LA. The lower campus, which is where I would go first before moving to the upper campus, happened to be where my mom went for twelve years back when it was the Westlake School for Girls. She came with me when I went in for my entrance interview and, crazy coincidence, one of her old teachers was interviewing me. He joked around, asking if I was anything like my mom—because, if I was, they'd need some luck. He told me stories about how she was known as a rebel because she embroidered her uniforms, wore platform shoes, and dyed her hair. She went against the grain and was never afraid to stand out. He made sure to add that she was a great student and everyone loved her all the same. It was just that she had her own way of thinking and expressing herself.

In that moment, I felt I was being honest by responding to his original question and saying I was nothing like that and they had nothing to worry about. But looking back, while I never had a rebellious stage like she did, I know that some of my boldness and ability to speak my mind must come from her. She was progressive, unafraid of what people said about her, and I respect that so much. If you were to put high-school versions of Jill and Lil side by side, we'd seem totally unrelated: the rebel and the good girl. But recently I've seen the similarities between us more and more, not only physically (we're pretty much twins, lucky me!), but also with our personalities. We have the same tenacious spirit, curious mind, and joy of meeting new people and experiencing new things.

Even though we couldn't have been more different as teenagers, Mom and I never failed to relate on some level to anything and everything when I was growing up. No topic was considered off-limits, so I always felt I could be honest. I remember the first day I got my period and had to ask her for help, the day I decided to start shaving, even the first time I wanted to wear a thong. Not to mention all those talks about school, boys, sex, drugs, alcohol—you know, *those* fun ones. She was a single mom raising a teenage daughter who had all kinds of questions. And because it was just the two of us, she took on the responsibility of addressing them all. That lifelong openness and ease in our conversations means that I now can talk to others effortlessly about things considered taboo or awkward. It also partly inspired my love of journalism, helped me find my voice and shape my opinions, and encouraged me to speak up, and, ultimately, to encourage other young people to do the same. I know that not every mother-daughter connection is like mine, but ours has taught me that no matter what kind of dynamic you have, open and honest conversation is key. Without it, we can't understand each other better. We can't connect. And it's when we truly connect that we come closer.

Of everything my mom has passed on to me, it's her words of wisdom that I'll never forget and always live by. "The quirky things that make you different are what make you beautiful," which I already mentioned, and "Consider the source and move on," which she learned from my grandmother, are two simple yet extremely poignant lessons that she's taught me and that I share with anyone who will listen. Through each of these mantras she encourages me to be me and to express myself however I choose. Embracing what makes you different is about accepting yourself for all that you are, flaws included. She has empowered me to be my own person, and even in my darkest times—during my eating disorders and bad relationships—she's stood by me and encouraged me. She was never afraid to voice her opinions, even if she knew I didn't want to hear them. This was especially true when I found myself so deep in that emotionally abusive relationship that I was blind to reality. Instead of forbidding me to see that guy, she listened and helped guide me to understand the situation and come to conclusions on my own. She encouraged me to consider who was treating me this way and what he was capable of, and to realize that I could never change him. And if someone isn't making me feel like the best version of myself, I should move on and find someone who will! There is no need to settle in this life and no need to be made to feel less than by someone else.

For all the incredible memories and joy our mother-daughter closeness has brought me over the years, it's also been difficult to navigate our relationship the older and more independent I've become. I started to really want a life of my own, one she didn't necessarily know all the details of. But the idea of separating myself while still remaining close baffled me. And it proved particularly tricky because we never had that typical period of separation when you leave for college. I moved out of the house when I was twenty, but I still lived just down the street from her. It may sound hypocritical, wanting distance but also wanting proximity—believe me, I still get confused about it all. And I'm not saying it's a bad thing! I loved being able to walk home!

It's just that it wasn't ideal for a healthy separation and instead helped foster the enmeshment between the two of us that formed from such an early age.

I remember feeling so guilty as a teenager if I had plans on the weekend because I didn't want to leave her alone. If I left, what would she do? She never put that pressure on me; it was something I put on myself. I think this dynamic is common in mother-daughter relationships as complex and close as ours. I felt this innate sense of responsibility to protect her from loneliness, much like her instincts to protect me. For me, that feeling of duty never went away as I became an adult: she was still the single mom who raised me, but I wanted to start experiencing things on my own. I needed to find my own voice. I never wanted physical distance to translate into emotional distance or to make her feel like I didn't want her involved or didn't care about her opinions. I'll always want that. But I'll also always want to have a separate existence, too.

I struggled in my initial efforts to pull away when I was sixteen, which was also the beginning of my eating disorders. As I neared the end of high school, Mom started dating someone, and I think I used the fact that she was occupied to justify hiding and lying about what I was going through. Her attention was no longer solely on me, and I took advantage of that. I stepped up my game and took care of myself so she could have a life of her own, and she believed I was okay. When she finally found out the extremes I'd gone to, she was devastated and blamed herself. She felt she had failed me as a mother. I never intended for that to happen, but how could it not? I had lied to my best friend, the person closest to me, who had always encouraged me to embrace myself and accept all my flaws as beautiful. I had believed what she said. And yet, driven by my own self-centeredness and sickness, I rejected her treasured wisdom and hurt her in the process. The last thing I ever wanted was for her to question what she had done wrong as a parent when all she had ever done was love and inspire me.

Needless to say, I don't know how I would have survived without having my mom's support, encouragement, and shoulder to lean on. Her advice has been invaluable and the life lessons I've learned are limitless. She's instilled in me a true appreciation for life, an acceptance of who I am, and a greater understanding of what it means to be a mother. Even if it took me rebelliously acting out in my own ways, I'm now very aware of everything I put her through when I was younger. But during it all, she continued to show such strength and love and, for that, I couldn't be prouder or more grateful. My mom's given up so much for me and if I'm lucky, I hope to one day grow up to be at least half the woman she is. One hell of a woman indeed.

Forever can be a beautiful thing. There's something so powerful about the way tattoos capture a moment in time for us to always remember.

7

EVERY TATTOO TELLS A STORY

When I think about a piece of art or a fashion designer's collection that I really love, I wonder why it speaks to me. Artists have their own intended meaning in everything they create, yet my personal experiences might make me see their work completely differently. And with time, our impressions can also change. We may find that what once compelled us no longer has relevance. What once captivated us no longer holds our interest. Art's ever-shifting nature is why I was both so keen and so scared to start getting tattoos. Once inked, the image is forever. As much as I might love a tattoo when I first got it done, what if I didn't like it in a week? A year? Twenty years? It's such a permanent expression and, as a kid, I wasn't a fan of permanence. I changed my mind a lot; I knew what I liked but I wasn't interested in sticking with one thing for too long. I loved changing my sense of style, how I decorated my room, and what I collected. The idea of forever scared me. It didn't seem possible for anything to last that long. Then again, since I was little, I had badly wanted to be inked, to treat my body as a canvas. There's something so powerful about the way tattoos capture a moment in time for us to always remember. They're an incredible form of artistic self-expression, unique markings that represent our personalities and tell our stories. They also have the ability to ground us even when we're moving around a lot. It's like bringing a piece of home with you wherever you go. Turns out, forever can be a beautiful thing!

My very first tattoo was done on my back in my own handwriting and says "Love Always and Forever" because I do believe that love can last a lifetime, whether it's with a partner, a friend, your family, or with yourself. Every one of my designs has a very personal meaning and most were inspired by the films I've worked on. All of them are also really finely drawn so they're easy to cover for work, something that would take hours if they had dark, heavy lines. I designed all of them myself, with occasional help from my mom and, of course, the tattoo artists themselves. I definitely got super lucky with my inaugural tatting experience, spoiled even, because I got to work with the genius that is Dr.

Woo. Not only is Woo's work unique, he's also the coolest guy. He's patient and collaborative, meshing my ideas with his artistic eye and attention to detail. I have so much fun with him that I never want to leave. And as soon as we're done, I'm ready to go back. Chances are, I've already gotten a couple more tattoos since writing this . . . ! I've been thinking about a swan or a seahorse for a while now, so who knows if they've both joined my collection. One, at the very least.

THE FACE OF SHOCK, NOT PAIN,
GETTING MY FIRST OF MANY PIECES BY DR. WOO.

Some of my tattoos were sketched weeks before walking into the shop, while others I chose only minutes ahead of time, and a few were planned but then changed at the last second when inspiration hit. Luckily, I love all of them! A week after I got my first tattoo, I booked my appointment for my second. I was hooked. When I went back, I got the one on my wrist, which is a special combo of a heart with the initials *LJ* which stand for my own name, Lily Jane, and also commemorates all the important people in my life whose names begin with J (and there's quite a few). The heart is surrounded by angels' wings and topped with the British crown, just in case anyone, myself included, needs a little reminder of my heritage.

THE ULTIMATE ARM CANDY.

After that, I made myself take a break and wait a year for my third (so hard!). When the time finally came and the urge had gotten the best of me, I had just wrapped *Love, Rosie*. While shooting in Dublin, I'd read a beautiful poem by Alice Walker and its title, "The Nature of This Flower is to Bloom," resonated so strongly with me. I wanted to incorporate the title with an actual flower and considered doing a lily but decided on a British rose instead as it fit nicely with Rosie, the name of my character in the film. The words, written in my handwriting, create the flower stem, and I included one falling petal to represent how I can be as delicate as a single petal yet as resilient and strong as the rose itself. I decided to get it on my foot because I could easily look at it and be reminded of its meaning. It also felt grounding to put it there, physically and emotionally, since the quote references what it means to grow, prosper, and come into our own.

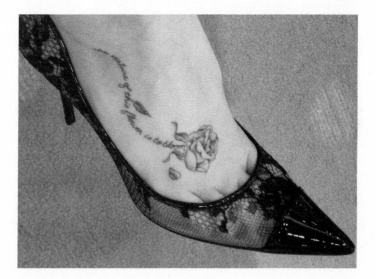

My fourth tattoo is on the left side of my body and extends under my left breast. It's a little fairy ballerina sitting on a moon, blowing on a dandelion whose floating seeds morph into a quote from American poet James Broughton: "True delicacy is not a fragile thing." The ballerina represents my beloved grandmother, Jane, who was a formally trained and well-respected dancer; the moon stands for all the times I've said "I love you to the moon and back" to my parents; the dandelion is about making a wish and sending it out into the universe, hoping one day it will come true; and the quote itself reminds me that being delicate, dainty, and sensitive doesn't mean you're not also strong and unbreakable. I can be everything. I am everything. I look at that tattoo every single day to remind myself how resilient and strong I am, especially while going through difficult times.

When I was filming the movie *Okja* in South Korea in the spring of 2016, I learned that tattooing in Seoul isn't exactly illegal, but you're supposed to be a licensed doctor to use tattoo needles. Which means getting a tattoo is a bit of a covert process there. So, naturally, it became my mission. I found an amazing artist named Doy whose work was so beautiful and whose thin lines and delicate aesthetic were very similar to my other pieces. The emotion in his designs was breathtaking and I just knew I had to have him ink a memory from my trip. My friend and I went together to his studio, which was worlds apart from any I'd ever visited. Instead of lots of people, loud music, and leather everywhere, he had burning candles, wood, and peace and quiet—that is, before we took over the stereo and blasted music to get us amped up. We were the only ones there and the vibe was so serene and relaxing I almost fell asleep! At this point, I'm just so used to the feeling that it doesn't hurt anymore. The whole experience was beautiful and spiritual, and my tattoo reflects that. It depicts a "water lily": a young woman (me) hugging herself sitting on top of the lily pad. I got it to commemorate *To the Bone,* the project I had just finished a month before, in which self-love and acceptance were two pivotal themes.

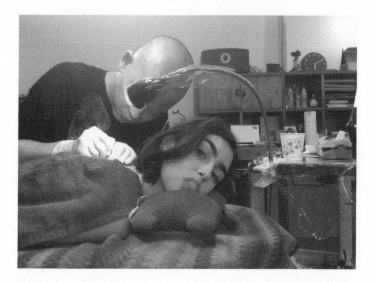

HAVING A BLAST WITH DOY, ONE TAT AT A TIME.

My tattoos aren't just beautiful works of art that I enjoy looking at; they're important reminders. They've become part of me, representing different chapters of my story and giving me a new sense of permanence. And although they may not be everyone's cup of tea, they are part of what makes me unique. And I love them. No matter how much of a paradox they make me!

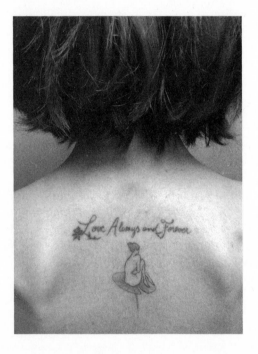

THE STORY'S JUST BEGINNING. STAY TUNED . . .

Don't live a boring life
if you can add a little
silly into it every once in
a while.

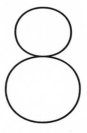

BE SILLY. IT'S ATTRACTIVE. NORMAL IS SO BORING.

've never been shy about being silly. Life's just too short for that. It's important to do the things you love, even if other people think they're weird. And who are they to say what's weird anyway? Do *they* set the cool standard? No. Doing what we love is what makes us unique. Goofball, nerd, dork, geek, nutcase, and eccentric are all nicknames I'll wear proudly if it means living each day laughing and smiling and being happy!

So here's a list of things that bring me joy, things that other people may judge me for or not understand. But I couldn't care less, because being silly Lily—uninhibited, spontaneous, fancy-free—is way more fun than being lame Lily. Life is often preplanned and micromanaged, so I welcome anything guaranteed to make me feel good on a daily basis.

1. I've always loved dressing up, whether it was for school plays, just for fun, or on Halloween. Before wearing costumes became part of my job, it was the best excuse to play a character and transform into someone else. And I took it very seriously! I never settled for those ready-made costumes that came in plastic wrapping (no disrespect). I'd scour vintage shops and accessory stores and rummage through my mom's closet to pull it all together.

I'VE CLEARLY NEVER SHIED AWAY FROM MIXING STYLES
OR MAKING A BOLD CHOICE.

I went to another level, planning weeks in advance and coming up with a whole wacky, complicated concept to run with. I once went dressed as the Fashion Police, decked out in mismatched patterns, a tool belt of accessories including a blow-dryer for victims of a bad hair day, and even citation tickets to hand out to offensive dressers, which, believe me, I used quite often that day.

AS THE OFFICIAL FASHION POLICE,
I THINK I SHOULD HAVE GIVEN MYSELF A TICKET.

2. Even after October has come and gone, my love of
    playing dress-up stays. Every spring, my friends and
    I go to the Renaissance Faire just outside LA. This
    highly anticipated annual tradition started with just me
    and my mom when I was younger, and I still wear the
    same outfit I bought at the faire when I was fourteen.
    Granted, it fits me a bit differently now . . . so I've
    gone from young princess to slightly older wench. But
    I have no shame rocking my look! I take pride in my
    dedication. We all run around shouting *Huzzah!* at the
    top of our lungs, eating corn on the cob and massive

pickles, taking pictures with every nymph we see, bowing to Queen Elizabeth and her maids in waiting, socializing with fellow enthusiasts, and cheering on the knights jousting and dueling "to the death." I don't care how silly it all sounds. I absolutely love it and wouldn't miss it for the world. Some of us have even gone so far as to fly back home from wherever we are in the world just to be able to make it. Now that's commitment.

THEN . . .

. . . NOW

3. Another thing I'm utterly dedicated to is Harry Potter.
    Each and every book. And every movie, too—I may
    have watched them all a hundred times, but if they're
    on TV I always become glued to the screen, reciting
    line after line pretending to be Hermione. There's just
    something about the whole franchise that makes me
    feel at home! It defined my childhood, inspiring me
    to disappear into the stories and go to a happy place.
    I remember my mom would be shopping somewhere
    and I'd just be in a corner on the floor, reading. As a
    kid, there were very few things I went crazy over or was

obsessed with, but I *was* that kid who waited in line for a book the day it came out and demanded to see each new movie the second it was released. I also may or may not have ridden on a broomstick wearing an official Quidditch cape when I visited the Warner Bros. Studio Tour in London. . . . I mean, how on earth could I have passed up that opportunity???

4. Among my many guilty pleasures is going to theme parks, especially Disneyland. If I could spend every day there, I think I would. Maybe it's because Disney makes me feel like an honorary kid or because I used to love pretending I was a fairy-tale princess (and sometimes still do . . .). No matter how old I am, I just can't get enough. I've celebrated many adult birthdays there and have zero shame about it. I adore everything about walking around the park, especially watching little kids experiencing it all for the first time, their wide-eyed stares as they meet the characters and go on all the rides. I love running around with my friends wearing Mickey ears, riding the roller coasters, screaming our heads off, and then watching the fireworks, completely in awe of how they create all that magic. I still treat each trip like it's my first, never sick

of the attractions. I refuse to let the experience get old and I cannot wait until I get to take my own kids one day and relive it all with them.

BELIEVE IT OR NOT, I STILL GET THIS EXCITED WHEN I SEE HER.

5. Going to flea markets is something I've been doing ever since my mom pushed me up and down the aisles in my stroller. In fact, I'd often find myself walking after a couple hours because she'd bought too many things and needed to wheel the rest. (Thanks, Mom!) We'd start in the wee early mornings, traversing the English countryside or LA when the sun wasn't even up and going to the bitter end when the vendors were hauling

away their remains. Sometimes when Mom and I stayed until closing, we'd even check the trash cans, driving by to see what was left behind by vendors who didn't want to have to lug everything back home. I know that may sound totally bizarre, not to mention dirty, but most of what we saw wasn't damaged at all and, if we hadn't claimed ownership, the items would've been hauled away anyway. And believe it or not, we've actually found some amazing keepsakes, including this incredible turquoise and gold beaded purse that I took home, cleaned up, and later brought to the Grammys with my dad the year he was nominated for "You'll Be in My Heart" from *Tarzan*. I got asked by someone on the red carpet where it was from. I cheekily said *La Poubelle* ("trash" in French) just to make it sound extra chic. Never was the saying "one man's trash is another man's treasure" more true, and I still have the purse in my closet to this day.

I used to think I'd grow up to hate antiquing because of how much I did it as a kid. But now I try to find markets and old shops everywhere I travel. I never tire of wandering around and keeping an eye out for things to collect. Who knows what incredible hidden gems I may find? I don't collect the same things anymore: gone are the days of Beanie Babies (a huge obsession!) and Spice Girls dolls (I had all of them!), endless sets of cool old keys, vintage metal lunch boxes, and Care Bears. But the thrill of the hunt still excites me just the same.

6. And here, in no particular order, are some other silly things that make me happy: I have a deep love of pickles; an obsession with apples; an appreciation for hot tea that's been sitting for hours and is now cold; a fascination with shadows; a tendency to look down instead of up when I'm walking so I can search for hidden street art; a compulsion to constantly apply hand sanitizer and hand cream throughout the day (I'm not a hypochondriac; I just like to be clean); an affection for black-and-white photography (everything seems more romantic in black and white); a habit of jumping in photos; the creation of what I like to call "makeup Monets" after cleaning my face with face wipes at the end of a night out; a collection of ticket stubs from movies, concerts, and museums since elementary school (I still have them all and can recount who I was with!); also a collection of fortune cookie fortunes because I think that keeping them will bring me luck; and, without fail, an impulse to sing in the car whenever a song comes on that I love even if I don't know the words. I'm also a huge lover of dancing, wherever and whenever. I never shy away from an empty dance floor. I think, "Well, someone has to be the first one. Why the hell not me?" I willingly, and

very often, compromise my cool factor basking under those strobe lights.

I TOLD YOU I WAS OBSESSED WITH PICKLES, EVEN ONES ON STICKS.

When all is said and done, I just love laughing. I love smiling and doing random, fun things with my friends and family. When we spend time with those who make us feel truly good and happy, we find that these quirks of ours, these things we enjoy doing, end up being the most endearing, attractive things about us. Being free and uninhibited is beautiful. Trying something new is invigorating. Don't live a boring life if you can add a little silly into it every once in a while.

Every one of us wants
our parents to tell us
how great we are; every
daughter needs to know
her dad loves her and
truly feel he means it.

A LETTER TO ALL DADS

Father-daughter relationships are very complex. We love our dads with all our hearts, but they can also drive us crazy. Sometimes they're overprotective; other times they don't show up for us at all. I've learned a great deal about myself from my own dad and, the older I get, the more I see how much our relationship has shaped me. But that doesn't mean we haven't had our challenges.

It isn't easy to talk to him about certain things—which I think is normal. Like many daughters, I struggle to voice my concerns and speak up because I don't want to upset my dad, weird him out, or disappoint him. We all create these images of ourselves based on what we think our dads want us to be. Growing up, I worried constantly about not living up to his expectations. I always tried to look my best, behave appropriately, and get good grades. And after crafting such a perfect picture of myself for so many years, that eventually became the norm. My hard work was expected rather than exceptional. It's not that my dad ever told me or even alluded to the fact that I was a failure, but my actions no longer got his unprompted attention or praise, so I constantly felt that I wasn't doing enough. That I wasn't enough. As daughters, we fight our way through adulthood trying to stay our dads' perfect little girls forever, but we also need to break out of that mold and do our own thing.

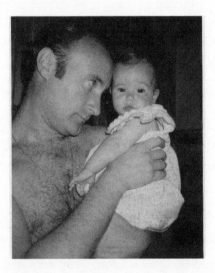

When I was five, my parents got divorced and my dad moved from our home in England to Switzerland, where he stayed for more than twenty years. He may have still been alive, but most of the time it felt as if he were completely gone. I knew he loved me, yet he wasn't physically around to tell me. I imagine it's similar to having a dad who lives with you and is emotionally unavailable. Whether physical or mental, absence affects a young kid. Every one of us wants our parents to tell us how great we are; every daughter needs to know her dad loves her and truly feel he means it. Because my dad was often gone, I never wanted to do anything that would make him stay away even longer. I became extra careful about what I said and how I said it, afraid he'd think I was angry or didn't love him. And the truth is, I *was* angry. I missed him and wanted him there. His absence was nothing I could control, nor was it something I understood, and that was so painful. I thought I needed to keep all those emotions to myself and never let him know. But that only created this terrible disconnect between us the older I got. All those years of hiding my feelings meant my dad wasn't good at reading me. He assumed everything was always fine because I never said otherwise. It established a detrimental pattern. And I've realized that many of my deepest insecurities stem from these issues with my dad. It's taken me more than a decade to resolve some of them (others I'm still resolving) and to finally build up the courage to speak my mind to him.

Although we as daughters all have personal experiences with our own dads, we can still relate to one another's feelings and frustrations on a broad level. We can help one another come to a deeper understanding and greater appreciation for our father-daughter relationships. Our dads may not always live up to our expectations of what we think they should be or do. We may even find that they aren't capable of giving us what we need. In those moments it's so important to remember that recognizing someone's flaws is a gift. It allows us to take a step back and reevaluate how we approach them and how to move forward. It also spares us the agony and pain of blaming ourselves for their actions. Once we've realized this, it's time to express our thoughts and feelings. We must let them know how much we still need them and how it's never too late to right wrongs or change patterns. It can get better for the both of us.

I'LL ALWAYS HAVE YOUR BACK.

But I know a conversation like that is never simple! Even if they're listening, sometimes our dads still don't truly hear what we're saying. So I've found that writing letters helps. Once our thoughts are on paper, our words and feelings can be expressed exactly how we want and they can be read and reread by the recipient. It's also an opportunity for a larger conversation, an open invitation for your dad to meet the emotionally mature, vocal side of you that's confident and strong. So feel free to read this letter to your dad or use it as a guide to write your own. I hope it makes expressing yourself a little easier. Remember, passion is universal and as long as your words are heartfelt and your intention genuine, he can't fault your bravery. All you can do is stay true to you and tell him how you feel.

Dear Dad,

No matter how old I get, I'll always be your little girl. No matter how mature I am (or like to think I am), I'll always value your opinion. I'll always need you. I'll always want you to check in with me no matter how much you think it will annoy me. Even if it does annoy me, I'll secretly love it. When I call you out on something that has upset or annoyed me, please don't mistake my criticism for loving you any less. Don't think that you've done something that can't be fixed. It's not about fixing; it's about moving forward knowing that things can change. I'm not counting up your past mistakes and keeping score and using them against you. I'm calling attention to the way certain actions make me feel and how they can be avoided going forward. It's important for us both to acknowledge not only the good things that make us happy, but also the unfortunate ones that hurt us. I want to celebrate my successes and share my failures with you, no matter how big or small. I know I'm technically an adult now but I still need your help. Want your help. And despite my best efforts to convince myself I don't need your approval, I still find myself seeking to be noticed, desperate for your hugs, craving your attention and affirmations. I still have those little-girl fears of saying something that might frustrate you. And I never want to let you down. But there will be times that I mess up. We all do it. Even you do it. But know that, even in all those "mess-ups," my intention was always to make you proud. I know you've told me that I do and that you love me. Still, it's nice to be reminded, especially when we're far apart. A quick call or even a short text or email to say hi every once in a while will do the job. Check in with me. You may think I'm busy, and I am busy, but even if I can't look at my phone for hours, at the end of the day I'd love to see that you were thinking of me. Because I'm definitely thinking of you.

Sometimes I try to be the bigger person, to take the high road, but you are the parent here. There are some things that I expect you to do—hope you would want to do—no matter how old I get. To be there to talk to, to learn from. To be someone who doesn't just show up for the fun stuff but is also there for the rough and tough and extremely-hard-to-deal-with stuff. We all make choices and, although I don't excuse some of yours, at the end of the day we can't rewrite the past. I'm learning how to accept your actions and vocalize how

*they made me feel. I accept and honor the sadness and anger
I felt toward the things you did or didn't do, did or didn't
give me. I've learned a lot and my eyes and heart are wide
open. I now understand that my frustrations surrounding our
communication are not about changing you but accepting you
as you are.*

*I, however, am changing. I'm getting to know who I
am, peeling back all the layers, and figuring out who I am
underneath everything. Finding my way out of dark times and
deciphering what makes me* me. *I'd like for you to meet who
I'm finding. I'd love for you to take the time to get to know
her and be part of that process. Because, I have to say, she's
pretty damn special. I forgive you for not always being there
when I needed and for not being the dad I expected. I forgive
the mistakes you made. And although it may seem like it's too
late, it's not. There's still so much time to move forward. And I
want to. I'm inviting you to join me. I love you with all of my
heart, more than you'll ever know, and am so thankful for you.*

I'll always be your little girl.

Love Always and Forever,
Me x

Sources of weakness can transform into your most important and influential sources of inner strength.

10

HARNESSING YOUR INNER
SUPERHERO

I'd like to introduce you to LiLi, a secret superhero. She's a be-spectacled, librarian-like, white-button-down-shirt-wearing, unassuming kinda lady at first glance—who kicks absolute ass with her intellect, charm, and heart when push comes to shove. She's the kind of woman who doesn't need a guy to fight her battles. Some may underestimate her abilities—and those are the ones she enjoys shocking the most.

Where on earth did LiLi come from? you may ask. Well, I cre-ated this superhero alter ego as a way to protect myself from . . . myself. LiLi appeared after years of work discovering my internal shadows—those feelings that cloud your perception of yourself and those critical little voices that lead you astray—and understanding the root of my physical and emotional insecurities. I used to see them all as negative, as things I was trying to eliminate. It took my incredible therapist pointing out that they didn't have to be bad for me to see their potential. I didn't have to treat them as weaknesses or obstacles. In a different light, they were positive attributes and, ultimately, superpowers. But the quest wasn't easy; oh no! It very rarely is for your average superhero. . . .

When I first moved to LA from England at age six, I had the strongest, cutest little British accent. But everyone in school made fun of me because I sounded different and didn't pronounce words or names like they did. All I wanted was to fit in, so I started listening to the other kids and mimicking how they spoke. I even did the same thing with movies, particularly *Peter Pan*. I would repeat Peter's dialogue to try to enunciate more clearly, more the American way. Looking back, I can't believe I wanted to get rid of that adorable accent! But at the time, I was so insecure. I just wanted everyone to like me and accept me. Now my ability to access my natural-born accent is a secret weapon I can whip out at a moment's notice. It's a total godsend! Not only is it a practical tool when I need to channel it for roles, like in *Love, Rosie*, but it's also an emotional one if I ever need to tap into the deepest parts of me. The first time I used it in a film was such an incredible experience. I felt more myself than ever.

And it came back so shockingly easily: all of a sudden I felt like little Lily from the countryside again, memories of home flooding back. I felt so natural. So right. And what had once made me feel insecure about sticking out in a new place now made me feel very much like *me*.

TO THIS DAY, IT'S STILL WHERE I FEEL MOST AT PEACE. MOST AT HOME.

Even though LiLi is a busy superhero, out there kicking butt and kicking down walls, she's still human and feels insecure about her appearance. I've always been very aware of the fact that I look young for my age. I know, I know! It's a blessing and I'll appreciate it when I'm older—a point I've been reminded of so many times. And now that I'm getting older, I *do* appreciate it. But growing up, the last thing I wanted was not to be taken seriously because people assumed I was young. Like the times I went into boardrooms and meetings at sixteen pitching talk show ideas. They wrote me off before even hearing what I had to say. My baby face also made auditioning for projects really tricky. I could very rarely play a character my actual age. Certain actors who were my age but looked way older set the standard for what a particular age "looked like" on screen. How would I ever be able to play their contemporaries? Because of this, I lost out on a lot of roles I wanted and more often had to consider ones that were younger.

The negative feedback and constant conversations about my appearance really got to me. I had heard it in boardrooms, in modeling castings, and now it was happening in film auditions. I still hear it today! And for a while, it made me feel completely stagnant, like I wasn't being allowed to mature. I let how people viewed me define how I viewed myself. But here's the thing: there's nothing I can do about the way I look. No amount of makeup or clothing will change it. I was wasting time on something out of my control, and I had to accept reality and finally put on my big-girl panties. So I did. Now I love shocking people when they find out how old I actually am. A woman once told me I looked fifteen when I was, in fact, more than ten years older! The expression on her face made me laugh, and I thanked her for it. Sure, it may have taken longer to transition into playing older characters, but in the meantime I continued playing the younger ones. And there have been some pivotal roles—Collins Tuohy, Snow White, and Clary Fray to name a few—that have really shaped me, and I wouldn't have been able to play them if I didn't look as young as I do. I no longer let any talk of age define how I feel about myself. Time is a gift, and I wonder why I ever wanted to speed it up. When it's gone, it's gone. And I want to make every moment count!

FROM MY UNIFORMED SCHOOL DAYS TO NOW: FOREVER THE PROUD STUDENT OF LIFE, EMBRACING THE UNFAMILIAR AND SOAKING IT ALL IN.

I like to think I have a big heart. I've always been a compassionate person who wears her feelings on her sleeve and puts others' needs before her own. It's an incredibly positive character-istic, but it also fed my insecurities around speaking up for myself in romantic relationships. As I've mentioned, I used to acquiesce to those I was dating because it was easier than using my voice. Taking care of a guy was my first priority above acknowledging what *I* needed. I was nervous that if they didn't like what I had to say or if I didn't give them what they wanted, they would leave. I put myself second for a very long time. I didn't value *my* heart's needs enough to voice them.

However, after dating a couple stand-up guys who I felt safe with and who told me not to be afraid to speak up, I learned that acknowledging my needs is just as important as acknowledging others'. And listening to my heart is one of the most powerful things I can do. It's how we understand and protect ourselves. It's how we learn to be the best possible partners, because we know exactly what it is we're looking for from someone else. Now I've made a promise to never silence myself or ignore my heart out of fear or insecurity. Our heart is our ultimate source of power. We can't forget that we need it in order to love ourselves so that we can then love others.

I used to overthink a lot of the time instead of just going with the flow. In dating, in work, in life. *Why didn't he call? What did I do? Why didn't I get that job? Could I have done something differently?* I didn't just stop at one question per situation, though. I'd completely obsess, sometimes driving myself crazy trying to predict the future so I could figure out exactly how to move forward. I never wanted to allow even the tiniest possibility of making a mistake. Logical and smart though that might seem, it didn't allow me to fully live in the present because I was so focused on the future. I developed a fear of letting go. The unknown scared me. This fear extended into my adulthood and still sometimes makes it hard to surrender myself and take risks, whether in the way I look or in how I perform in my job, because I can't control what will happen. I can't know the outcome, and that scares me. Taking risks equals messing up, which equals negative attention. So why would I ever want to take risks if it would end badly? I could look foolish or "un-Lily." What will people think?

As much as I'd love to say I don't worry about people's views of me, I do. It's inevitable. It's human. But by understanding my tendency to overthink, I've learned that the most important person to please at the end of the day is myself. As long as I'm happy and proud, that's all that matters. Letting go doesn't have to be such a scary thing. In fact, it's when some of life's most beautiful, magical moments happen.

Another positive thing that emerged from my tendency to overthink and be ultra-attuned to situations is that I became a great judge of character and extremely good at reading people. Having so closely observed people's behavior over the years, I can handle myself in all types of settings, around all types of human beings. I've developed a protective covering around my heart that shields it from others' judgments and deflects their emotional projections. I try not to let what they say or think get to me. And because I feel more grounded and solid in who I am, I don't fear how letting go will make me look in front of them. Now I can use those skills—which were a direct result of my insecurity—to properly assess individuals (potential suitors included!), better live in the moment, and feel free to step outside my comfort zone. In this sense, my knowledge became power.

Through all these experiences—being ridiculed for my accent, being underestimated as a young person, not speaking up in relationships, and overthinking because I don't want to mess up—and what I've learned along the way, I've come to realize that sources of weakness can transform into your most important and influential sources of inner strength. Our insecurities and shadows, whether physical or emotional, shouldn't rule our lives or dictate how we view ourselves. Instead, we should harness them to our advantage. Use them. After all, they never fully go away. They're the parts of ourselves that can bring out the best in us if we just learn how to properly work *with* them as opposed to against them. They can be our partners in crime, our sidekicks. After all, LiLi may be a superhero, but she could always do with a little extra help to save the day.

You have to love yourself the most and use your voice. But when I used mine, I was talking to his addiction and it refused to hear me.

11

IN A RELATIONSHIP WITH ADDICTION

Dating an addict is incredibly difficult. Believe me, I've done it. There were the guys who'd go to the bathroom multiple times during dates, blaming weak bladders. Others who would disappear for days at a time, lost on a bender. There was even one ex-boyfriend whose denial of his drinking problem and subsequent attempts at sobriety crippled my trust and destroyed our relationship from the inside out. Then there was my dad. His battle with alcoholism, and my fear that he wouldn't survive, forever altered my own relationship with drinking and forced me to see the destructive patterns I was forming in my dating life. It forced me to wake up, take charge, and make a change.

I know that I am not perfect. I am well aware that I've been guilty of turning to my own self-destructive habits in the past. I dealt with my insecurities about my body by adopting unhealthy compulsions like obsessing over what I ate and how to get rid of it. My addiction was to food (or lack thereof) and exercise. But never drinking or drugs. I've had fun, wild nights out with friends, but liquor for me isn't a form of rebellion or a means of escape. Drinking for the sake of getting drunk just doesn't interest me. For me, substances are about moderation, judging the appropriate time and place and listening to myself to know when enough is enough. I'm not comparing addictions, and I'm not saying one is more justified. Having never had an unhealthy relationship with drugs or drinking, I'm simply admitting I can't relate. What I *can* relate to, however, is the experience of being controlled by something that feels out of your control. But unlike some of my exes, I chose to own my issues, putting them out there as something I'm working on, not ignoring or hiding.

After finding myself in toxic relationships that left me hurt and confused, time and time again, I began to wonder what it was about *me*. Maybe these guys saw me as someone who would put up with their needs, or placate them, or not make them face whatever it was that drinking or drugs helped them avoid. Maybe they saw me as nice and easy to dupe. No matter the reason, the bottom line is: they didn't regard me highly enough. Didn't respect me enough. They took advantage of the fact that I saw the best in them and gave them the benefit of the doubt. Their lies went straight over my head. All I heard were passionate declarations and grand plans for our future (which they'd typically forget once they were sober). It seemed like they were constantly switching their feelings on and off—and that part was the hardest. The reality was, I was just a cover for them. I fit the image of what their parents and friends approved of, yet had absolutely no clue about their double life. Call me naive, but when those guys dropped me home at the end of the night, I didn't realize they were about to start round two of their evening. They were desperate to be under the influence and I didn't even notice. I'd had no idea it was their addiction talking.

So why was I attracted to similar types of partners with addiction issues? Why was I drawn to their erratic behavior and their lies and their bullshit? Well, we as women are often born nurturers. We think that we can help our partners and bring out the best in them. That we can bring about change and inspire hope. Although we do a damn good job most of the time, when the other person is incapable of seeing it themselves, it's just not possible. And the more we try, the more we're dragged down with them. We sacrifice our well-being because we believe we can be the person to save the ones we love. I've been guilty of this fixing mentality over and over, both with boyfriends and family members—which is not a coincidence. I'm drawn to guys like my dad who are creative, sensitive, and somewhat mysterious. The mystery is intriguing and exciting because you never know what mood they'll be in or what they'll do. But that lack of consistency wasn't a good thing for me. It wasn't healthy. As high as their highs were, their lows were always lower. Moments of lightness and joy quickly turned to darkness. Out came their demons, vices, and addictions. And I had to be the one to put my foot down and say no when they were incapable of doing it themselves. I tried to help and they threw that help back in my face far too many times. Facing it alone got frustrating and tiring. Ultimately I decided these men were too emotionally dangerous and unhealthy for me. I couldn't do it anymore so I decided to put a stop to it and reevaluate my dating cycle.

The hardest of all these relationships was with an ex-boyfriend who used substances as a way to self-medicate. (The same guy who ghosted me after I called him out on his addiction.) I loved him so incredibly much and believed in him more than anyone. We went through many phases in our relationship, alternating between the best moments of my life and feeling more pain than I thought possible. At the beginning of our relationship, he was completely sober, having made the decision months before to quit everything and kick-start a healthy lifestyle. We coexisted beautifully and it all seemed to be going well. Then he decided to reincorporate alcohol into his life and I started to see a shift. He was often on edge and extremely sensitive. Part of the problem was that he couldn't have just one or two drinks. And when he drank to excess, he worried about everything. He doubted things I'd say and became incredibly insecure. I found myself constantly reassuring him of my affections, and there came a point when nothing I said could make him feel better. His self-doubt and self-hatred would creep in and he'd drink and drink to ignore what was really bothering him. In public, though, his insecurities never showed. He was fun and loving when he drank. Always the life of the party. Never one to get angry or volatile. But as great as he'd feel for that short period of time, I could see his paranoia and extreme lows coming from a mile away. And there was little I could do to prevent them. I discouraged the drinking but I also didn't want to mother him. I had no interest in controlling him or pressuring him to be someone other than who he was. I just wanted the best for him, for him to be truly happy and healthy.

In the end, his denial of his drinking problem put too great a strain on our relationship. I saw so clearly what it did to him and how it made him feel. And, in turn, how awful it made me feel. His loving gestures and words often unsettled me because I didn't know if they were real or liquid courage. I understand that sometimes a little buzz makes you feel bolder about saying or doing things. But it can't be all the time. When it got to the point where I wasn't capable of helping him anymore, I suggested he get outside help. Even though the last thing I wanted was for him to be angry at me and feel abandoned, that's exactly how he felt. He thought I'd given up on him, despite it being the exact opposite: I believed in him so much that I couldn't bear watching him waste his time, his energy, his life. I was in a relationship with his addiction, and I wasn't a healthy version of myself. I knew I was making the right choice by breaking up; I also knew how much I loved him. I hoped one day maybe we'd make it work again, under different circumstances. But there was no way he could understand any of that in his state. It tore me apart.

I decided we needed to take a break to focus on ourselves and maybe, after that, we could function better as a couple. During that time, he got help and took it very seriously. When I saw him again for the first time since out breakup, I could tell he'd made a huge effort and become more clear-minded, aware, and solid. He also finally acknowledged his alcoholism, a huge and powerful moment. I believed in him, believed in the changes he'd made, and, despite our past issues, our love was undeniable. I saw immense hope in our future. He was sober and seeking the help he knew he needed and wanted to work through his addiction. So why, after all that, didn't our relationship have a fairy-tale ending? To this day, I'm still not sure. My main problem was that, yes, he was sober, but he'd started drinking nonalcoholic beers to excess instead. He was just substituting one vice for another, not dealing with the root of the problem. Having done something similar with my own addictions, I knew what it was like to Band-Aid a situation by distracting yourself with something else. It takes the focus off the main issue. In his case, not drinking was half the battle. The other half was facing why he felt the need to drink in the first place. And because he stopped reaching out for help and going to support groups regularly, he still suffered from the anxiety and insecurities he once had. I noticed small changes in his demeanor as the old ways crept back in. This time, however, I knew myself and our old triggers better and was more vocal about my concerns. I encouraged him again to seek out the professional support he needed. But the second I brought it up, he disappeared and I never heard from him again.

When I used to look back on this bizarre ending to our relationship, I felt like maybe I'd said the wrong thing or went about it in the wrong way. I felt guilty about breaking up the first time and weak for not being able to fix the situation the second time. But then I have to remind myself that it wasn't me who drove him to make his choices. It was him. His actions were loud and clear, and his final, absolute silence spoke volumes. I couldn't fix him. He'll forever hold a special place in my heart and I'll always want to protect him, but no matter how much I loved or always will love him, my love alone couldn't counteract his lack of self-love. I had coped with his issues the best I could and I no longer regret how I handled the situation or how I handled myself. I trusted my gut and how I felt, and I never gave up on him. I still haven't. I just realized what was unhealthy for me and then set boundaries. I valued myself in a way that meant not compromising my health for someone else. And that isn't selfish or something to feel guilty about. It's smart. You have to love yourself the most and use your voice. And I now recognize that when I used mine, I wasn't talking to him. I was talking to his addiction and it refused to hear me.

Dealing with my ex's battle with alcohol prepared me for the future in ways I didn't expect, specifically when I finally recognized my own father's get worse and worse. I hadn't become fully aware of my dad's drinking until it developed into a serious problem in my early twenties. I was in my late teens when it started, but at that time I hadn't yet dated anyone with addiction problems and didn't know what it looked like. Once I was aware, it was all I could see. I noticed how good he'd been at hiding it, an ability I'd acquired with my disordered eating. I was constantly afraid something would happen to my dad. No matter what I said or how much I expressed my concerns to him, the drinking continued. I saw it being used as a tool, as a coping mechanism. I was convinced that one day I would wake up to a phone call from halfway across the world saying that it had finally gone too far.

Fortunately, after numerous appeals from me, my siblings, and his close friends, my dad took control of the situation and has now been sober for several years. I never gave up on him. Even if my constant efforts got annoying, my determination never faltered, and my heart remained hopeful. I kept saying there was so much to look forward to, so many things I still needed him for, like walking me down the aisle at my wedding and meeting his grandchildren.

Just as it had been with my ex-boyfriend, intervening and speaking up like that was one of the most difficult, frustrating, and painful things I'd ever had to do. And one of the hardest parts was that it was out of my control. And for someone like me who loves to be in control, that was torture. I learned that when an outside substance is being used as a means to cope or mask something greater, the drinking or drug use cannot stop until the person understands and accepts what it is they're trying to hide from. Not dealing with the root of the problem means they'll never get better. My dad couldn't acknowledge he needed to stop until he wanted it for himself. I could only do so much. And I needed to see that.

It's no big surprise after all these experiences that I developed trust issues. For a long time I doubted any man who complimented me while drinking. I couldn't accept words of endearment without wondering whether it was the guy or the substance talking. All conversations and interactions required second-guessing. Maybe he didn't actually want to travel with me or have me meet his friends and family after all. Maybe he didn't love me. Maybe he didn't even really like me that much in the end. Even with guys who didn't have an alcohol problem, their being slightly tipsy and saying nice things made my skin crawl. The fear became poisonous, ruining a lot of potentially genuine and lovely moments. Now I try hard not to project my past experiences onto others. I can't control how someone else handles themselves. And I can't live my life doubting everything that people say to me.

Being in relationships with addiction prevented me from being in actual, progressive relationships with those addicted. At the end of the day, the more they refused to admit their problem, the more I was the one who suffered. Who doubted if I'd done enough. Been enough. Where did I stand? Why did they keep disappearing or relying on substances? What were they escaping from? I felt dumb and disrespected. I felt foolish. And yet I know now that these experiences made me stronger and far more aware. My eyes are open wide. I know myself better than ever before and I trust my instincts when they warn me something isn't quite right. I don't want to find myself back in a situation where I'm being duped or taken advantage of. Plus, it hurts too much to be invested in someone who would rather master the art of self-destruction then face their problems and admit they need help. Asking for help is never a sign of weakness. It's one of the bravest things you can do. And it can save your life.

I now view food as energy for my mind and body rather than something to be scared of. Because without it, I can't grow stronger—emotionally, mentally, or physically.

FOOD AS FUEL, NOT PUNISHMENT

"Love is the most important ingredient"—it's a tad corny, but entirely true. Cooking from the heart is what makes the ultimate soul food, the dishes we can't live without. For a long time I didn't understand that. I didn't recognize the importance of feeding myself, body and mind. It took me decades to come around to cooking, to see it as powerful rather than terrifying. As a kid I enjoyed spending time in the kitchen and trying my mom's homemade meals. Being together as we ate and chatted about our days then watching our favorite TV shows during dessert was something I looked forward to. But even though I loved the rituals associated with cooking, I didn't make an effort to do it myself. A lot of my friends baked from an early age and brought delicious confections to school for bake sales or as surprise treats. Not me. Then cut to high school, at the height of my struggle with eating disorders, and needless to say learning to cook was still not at the top of my list. It wasn't until my early twenties, after I really started coming to terms with my food issues and was dating a guy I truly loved, that I decided to change.

LOST IN THE KITCHEN FROM DAY ONE.

At my core, I wanted to be able to take care of the people I loved and to give them comfort. There's a certain strength in providing for someone else, and I wanted to feel strong. I had long had this idea of becoming the epitome of womanliness in the sense of nurturing and providing sustenance, and I became determined to finally make that happen. Coincidentally, my boyfriend at the time was the first guy I ever imagined being with for a long time, maybe even marrying, and I wanted to get a head start on perfecting some life skills I'd neglected. Plus, baking for him could create a new and positive association with food and bring back the fun, social elements I used to love about it. More than anything, the whole endeavor was something *I* was actively choosing, something that would allow me to regain some of the control that my disorder had had for far too long. I finally felt confident and brave enough to take the plunge.

To better explain the roles food and cooking have played throughout my life, I'm going to back up a bit. For starters, food really did occupy such a happy place in my childhood, and I have only the most positive memories of it. I spent my years in England surrounded by farms and local produce. I have recollections of amazing English delicacies, neighborhood pubs, and culinary traditions. And when we moved to LA, Mom and I made a weekly habit of supermarket shopping together. I'd accompany her every Monday after school and we'd menu plan for the week and say hi to all our friends who worked there. It became one of our local hot spots. Shopping turned into an event, free cookies and samples included. Same idea whenever we went back to visit England. One of the first things we always did was drive straight to the market and stock up on all the things we'd missed, our comfort foods: sharp farmhouse cheddar cheese, Marmite, pickled onions, chocolate digestives, Jaffa Cakes, hot cross buns, sausages. I'd run around alternately grabbing snacks off the shelves and spending minutes just standing and staring at all the options. We'd spend what felt like hours discussing ingredients and deciding on dinner plans. Afterward we'd go home and I'd sit at the kitchen table taking in all the sights and smells as she cooked. Then, like clockwork, no matter how big our dinner, we'd both wake up in the middle of the night for the first couple of nights and have baked beans on toast with tea and biscuits. It became our staple cure for getting over jet lag. Food was an enjoyment, a cure, a positive thing.

Perhaps because it was such a foreign skill to me, I was also fascinated by the science and process of cooking, whether in person or on TV. I've been a massive fan of cooking shows ever since *Top Chef* debuted. I'd watch episode after episode of every culinary competition imaginable, salivating over the expertly prepared platters and plates. The chefs used ingredients I'd never heard of in ways I'd never imagined, and their creativity and passion were infectious. I also started learning about vegan options and was intrigued by how certain dishes looked so simple to construct yet tasted so amazing. Substitutions didn't have to mean you skipped out on flavor. I'd spend forever eyeing countless cookbooks in my favorite bookshops, many of which now line the countertop in my kitchen, and I even read a novel called *Eat Cake* over one summer vacation. It was the story of a woman who started a cake-baking business late in life and how the journey forever changed her, emotionally and physically. I remember thinking: If she could just start experimenting, why couldn't I?

Well, I'll tell you: my eating disorders wouldn't let me. Once anorexia and bulimia took over my life, God forbid I allow myself a treat every once in a while, let alone put something in my mouth that I didn't know the exact ingredients or calorie count of. Regulating my food intake was already stressful enough without the addition of trying new things. My anxiety surrounding what I did or didn't eat turned into a fear of letting go, and my laissez-faire attitude around trying and sampling everything ceased to exist. But there were some habits I couldn't shake, and I still found myself spending ages standing in the grocery aisles staring at all the different items—it was just that, now, they were all off-limits items and what was once pleasurable became a self-inflicted torture.

Then there came a day, after battling long and hard with my disorder, that I couldn't take it anymore. I'd had enough of feeling controlled by food. Of being terrified to eat certain things because I thought they'd make me fat or because I'd feel guilty for treating myself. And I was sick of feeling powerless in my kitchen, of aimlessly flipping through food magazines and arriving empty-handed at parties. It was ridiculous to be a twenty-four-year-old and not know my way around a kitchen. I needed and wanted to be more self-reliant. So I gathered all my appliances' instruction booklets and schooled myself on their inner workings, from on and off switches to all the specialized settings. Then I sat in front of my computer for ages and Googled all sorts of recipes. My boyfriend at the time, who had partially inspired this endeavor, was on a gluten-free diet, and I wanted to be able to satisfy his new dietary restrictions, which meant the staples of traditional baking were no-nos. And while I was at it, why not make it even more of a challenge by cooking gluten-free AND vegan! Maybe religiously watching all of those cooking shows would finally pay off! Even if they didn't, I've never been someone to take the easy route—why start now?

After printing out a bunch of recipes that looked delicious and easy enough, I headed out to run 1,000 errands. I didn't tell anyone what I was up to just in case I failed epically. I didn't feel like setting myself up for even more added pressure. (I do a pretty good job of adding that on my own. . . .) I walked into a restaurant supply store with a list of the utensils I needed and went on a shopping rampage. The hardest thing about a place like that is, all of a sudden, you start to convince yourself you need things you've never even heard of. Who knows, maybe I'll need an individual avocado peeler! Or ten nozzles to ice cupcakes! Or a self-heating butter knife! Fifteen different-sized baking trays! A measuring spoon shaped like an elephant! But I kept my blinders on as best as I could and focused on what I really needed for my planned dishes. Once my hands were full, I paid and bounded out the door to the market.

NOW HERE'S ONE UTENSIL I COULDN'T LIVE WITHOUT.

Now, exploring the supermarket was a whole other—and new—beast. I scoured the shelves, which, even just a few weeks earlier, I would've stared at longingly but never dared select anything from. I asked various employees where certain ingredients were and sometimes even *what* they were because I didn't recognize the gluten-free ones. It was like a maze in there, but once I made it through, I felt even more accomplished. All I needed now was to put it all together and hope I didn't start a fire!

I went home, unloaded my bags, and got to work. I separated everything by dish and created my schedule. My mission was simple: create a multicourse dinner for my mom. I didn't tell her she was going to be my official taste-tester because I really wanted it to be a surprise. And, to be honest, I didn't want her checking in on my progress. The menu was homemade guacamole and chips; a chilled quinoa salad with onions, tomatoes, cucumber, and garlic; and salmon in a foil sachet steamed with vegetables, herbs, lemon, and agave. For dessert: the chocolate chip quinoa cookies that would quite soon become my specialty.

I laid everything out, set timers, put on some music, and took off full steam ahead. And you know what? I owned the shit out of that kitchen. It may have taken me three hours to perfect everything, but I'm super proud to say I didn't mess anything up. I tested everything as I went and seasoned accordingly. I couldn't believe that it was all working! That I, Lily, classified fool in the kitchen, was actually dominating every recipe.

THE MASTER BAKER HARD AT WORK:
MUFFIN MANIA IN THE ENGLISH COUNTRYSIDE.

By the time I got to the cookies, my confidence was soaring. My oven didn't know what it was in for. I made the dough and let it set in the fridge for forty minutes while I cleaned up my counters and put everything away. Then I rolled individual balls of gooey goodness and placed them carefully on two trays, put them in the oven, closed the door, and prayed. I don't think my eyes ever left that glass door. I snuck a sniff every once in a while and the smell alone was enough to make me giddy. Finally they finished baking and I let them cool as I gathered all my dishes into containers and called my mom to tell her I was driving over with a surprise. Before I left, I took a minute to close my eyes and take a bite of a cookie. I don't think I could ever fairly describe how meaningful that moment was—how, in one second, that single bite changed my life. The consistency, taste, and temperature all combined to create the most delicious mouthful. I know this probably sounds so strange and quite insignificant to those thinking, "It's just a cookie, girl. What's the big deal?" But for someone who had feared desserts for so long and felt guilty for even *considering* baking them, a cookie that tasted *that* good that *I* had made was beyond. I was so proud. I had faced a fear head-on and won.

THE EPIC BATCH OF QUINOA CHOCOLATE CHIP COOKIES
THAT CHANGED MY LIFE.

So, off I went to share my success with my mom! I couldn't wait to see her reaction. When I opened the door and handed her a stack of Tupperware and told her I'd made her dinner, she just looked at me and laughed. I repeated myself and opened up all the containers. She went silent. Remember: in all her twenty-four years of motherhood, she had never seen me so much as make toast. She gamely grabbed a plate, dished it all out, picked up her fork, and took her first bite. And you know what? She LOVED it! It took her a few minutes to believe that I had indeed cooked it all, but when it finally hit home, she couldn't stop raving. As curious as I was to stay and see her finish off every last bite, I didn't. But I did make her jump ahead to dessert quickly and taste a cookie before I left, which she absolutely loved, too! To this day she requests them regularly, as do a lot of my friends.

My countless hours slaving away in the kitchen that day were worth it. I kick-started an obsession that has truly changed my life and my perspective on food. It's become a gateway to so much more exploration. I constantly Google recipes just for fun, for dinner parties, and for holidays. I never would have thought that my mom's kitchen in LA, the one where I used to watch her cook, would now house the many treats I bring her. It even changed the way I viewed my kitchen in the house where I grew up in England. Whenever we visit, I no longer just sit around reading at the kitchen table. Instead, during the Christmas holiday, I partake in the annual feast with dishes of my own, including my Christmas spice cake. I take days to prepare and plan very seriously, and don't get me started on decorating.

I even started baking treats while I was away on location filming: brownies, cupcakes, muffins, breads, macaroons, cakes, doughnuts, and pies. It became a form of therapy, a way for me to escape. With every passing day comes progress with my disorders; with every new cooking attempt comes a particular set of lessons. Not all my dishes pan out or look identical to the images online, but they're always filled with love and hard work, and that's what matters.

I may have started out experimenting in the kitchen for a guy, but those days are long gone. Now I do it because it makes me feel good. It gives me time to myself where I can zone out and be creative. There's a sense of calm I get from following a set of steps knowing what the end result will be, but also a sense of freedom when I deviate and improvise. Succeeding is special and momentous. But I also quickly came to terms with failing in the kitchen because sometimes you just don't get the proportions right and what you think is a fabulous idea is actually a major disaster. It's in those moments I learn from my mistakes and know better for next time. It helps me let go, be more free, and banish feelings of guilt and shame surrounding what I eat. I now view food as energy for my mind and body rather than something to be scared of. It's fuel, not punishment. Because without it, I can't grow stronger, emotionally, mentally, and physically. Plus, it's so nice to treat myself and reap the benefits of my own creations. My little brothers even love my baking and that's saying something because getting kids to enjoy "healthy" alternatives isn't always easy, especially when they involve vegan chocolate. I now get requests from friends in different cities, even different countries, to bring containers of baked goods when I travel. Baking has become a gift to myself and to so many others. I guess you could say I have officially become *that* girl, a bona fide master baker who is now more empowered than controlled by food.

#PRIORITIES

Choosing how and when to admit my truths allows me to take back the power that my insecurities had once stolen.

SPILLING OUR SECRETS

t's no secret that we as women all want to look and feel our best. But what *is* a secret is how insecure this pressure can make us feel. We claim to know that every woman feels this way and yet we're still surprised when another girl—particularly a celebrity—openly admits it. Maybe certain concerns, or even "weaknesses," seem too taboo and lame to discuss, especially when looking good is supposed to be effortless. But if we just released our fears into the open and spoke about them freely, I think we'd all feel better.

We all know what it's like to be a woman in the twenty-first century. We may each have different experiences, but no matter what our particular journey is, we know about grueling workouts and conscious eating patterns. This is why I assumed it was obvious that I face the same body insecurities and self-consciousness as other women around the world. Evidently, it's not obvious at all! So I want to spill my secrets to you.

It was a recent conversation with a friend's fourteen-year-old daughter—whom I'll call Grace—that first opened my eyes to this misconception. I realized that by not talking about these insecurities and how I face them on a daily basis, it seems like I don't have them at all. Grace and I started our chat by talking about fashion and school, and then we happened to segue into food and exercise. She opened up right away, expressing her frustration about not looking like the girls she saw in magazines. She told me how annoying it was that they didn't have to work hard at how they looked and that they never felt ashamed of themselves—a theory she'd come to wholeheartedly believe after reading several articles where actresses spoke about never dieting and hating exercise. Grace said that it appeared to her, and to all her friends, as though the models and actresses they admired were all born skinny and perfect.

First of all, I don't care who you are or what you do: no one is perfect. Perfection is an unattainable goal, a concept that took me a while to figure out, having harmed myself trying to reach it at a young age. And the fact that this strong, beautiful girl believed that anyone she saw in magazines, including myself, was perfect—well, that had me completely disturbed. How could she and her friends think I was above having insecurities and feeling self-conscious? And even worse, how could they think that I woke up every day, ate cheeseburgers (I don't even eat red meat), boycotted the gym, and still looked the way I do (which, by the way, isn't any more special than the next woman)? But she did. She was letting the impossible standard set by the media determine her own self-worth. And staring into her eyes, I could see it was making her distressed and disheartened. Now, that was some serious bullshit.

The moment Grace was done talking, I jumped at the chance to hug her. And to say how utterly wrong she had it. Ever since I can remember, I have worked so very hard to feel confident about myself. The last thing I'd ever want is for her to feel less than or bad about herself based on a false perception of me. Especially because I see so much of myself at that age reflected in her.

When I was fourteen, I was so confused about how to feel in my own skin, how to balance allowing my body to grow but wanting to control it, how to quiet the voices in my head telling me I wasn't pretty enough, thin enough, good enough. I think back on that time and know I was far too young to be worried about all that. I shouldn't have been so concerned with how I looked or how to deprive myself. I didn't fully allow myself to just be a kid and let nature run its course. So I sure as hell wasn't about to allow my young friend to do the same.

I was determined to make sure Grace knew that we all experience these concerns and that there's no magic filter separating those found in magazines and those reading them. After all, I still find myself looking through magazines and comparing myself to the photos, despite knowing the amount of Photoshop and tweaking they've been through. I'm still influenced and impacted by these images and by the things I read, including those same interviews about actresses hating the gym and eating whatever they want. Even though I know *full well* their purpose is to create a certain image.

While talking to Grace about all the important things in life to focus on instead—like maintaining a healthy lifestyle, being aware of our needs and knowing what fuel to feed our bodies, and less frequently using words like "dieting" when talking about food—I also admitted that my hyperawareness of all these things had, at times, played too pivotal a role as I was growing up. It got in the way of savoring the moment, being present, and enjoying life.

I can't change my past, nor would I want to. All I can do now is move forward, apply what I've learned, and pass any wisdom along to Grace and other young women who may not even know they need to hear it. Though I don't think my body issues will ever fully go away, I am definitely more aware of them now and view them in a different light. I eat well and work out to feel stronger and healthier, and to look my best for myself—not for everyone else. I've learned not to let concerns about body image or perception or other people control me. Instead, I surround myself with positive and uplifting women who help me focus on encouraging, inspiring, and empowering myself to work harder. Because feeling good in my own skin is the ultimate payoff.

When we finished the rest of our conversation, the look in Grace's eyes was priceless. I saw this immense weight lift from her shoulders, and I could feel the relief emanating from her. I strangely felt lighter, too. I felt exhilarated. I realized in that moment, by talking to her, I had been talking to my younger self. I was imploring fourteen-year-old Lily to let go of her self-doubt, to embrace who she was, and to welcome absolute, pure freedom.

I count myself lucky to have had this opportunity to reveal my truth, because it not only brought Grace and me closer, it also taught me a lot about myself. I wish that, when I was a teenager, I'd had someone to talk to and relate to who was my age and who was battling the same things I was. Anxieties and issues don't just disappear if we don't talk about them. In fact, we can't fully deal with them if we don't open up. My chat with Grace reminded me just how much the media has always played a huge role in the way I've seen myself in comparison to other women and in the way other women see me. And I'm now more aware than ever how fine the line between truth and fiction really is. Even when I think I have some semblance of control over how I'm perceived, I don't. It's encouraged me to be even more honest with myself about my insecurities and to be open to sharing them with others.

Maybe if I'd only shared more at Grace's age, I wouldn't have felt like I was going through these things alone. Choosing how and when to admit my truths now allows me to take back the power that my insecurities had once stolen. I will no longer let them dictate how I live my life. After all, bottling up my secrets never did any good. If I'd just spilled them to someone I trusted, I could have felt more connected and supported. And that's what it's all about.

By sharing, we learn that we're not alone, that we're not so different after all. We're all human. We all want to feel part of something greater.

14

TALK MORE, CREATE CONNECTIONS

I think it's amazing just how much we can each relate to another person, even strangers, when we're willing to open up and share. I can't count the number of times I've been in random groups of people where we end up bonding over mutual romantic struggles, family issues, or everyday fears. It's what being alive is all about: going through similar things, sharing familiar experiences, and feeling the same feelings. We're all human. We all want to feel part of something greater. But sometimes, though we recognize this shared instinct to connect, we get stuck in our own heads, convincing ourselves that no one else could understand our problems, that we're outsiders. We become our own worst enemies and retreat inward—but that kind of self-isolating makes it harder for others to reach out just when we need it most.

Instead, I've found it's better to talk to someone about what's going on; it alleviates my stress and fear because, chances are, they know what I'm going through. Maybe they've been there, too, or have a friend who has. By listening and demonstrating their understanding, they help me gather my thoughts and feel calmer, just as I did with Grace.

A conversation can't start unless someone speaks up. For that to happen, we must feel protected, and fostering a safe environment is crucial. It doesn't matter if it's a room of two people or two hundred, without that space and freedom, we can't fully open up. At Harvard-Westlake I was part of a voluntary program called Peer Support. It was made up of randomly selected groups of two student leaders, two student trainees, and a handful of students, and we met every Monday for two hours in assigned classrooms. I participated in tenth, eleventh, and twelfth grades, and the supportive environment inspired me to open up and channel my love of listening and connecting. I gained the confidence to share a lot about myself and encouraged others to do the same. I became good at lending support and helping quieter students use their voices. It never felt clinical or intimidating and, since there were no adults and everything was kept confidential, we were all less guarded and less on edge. You might think that whole secrecy rule would be completely ignored—after all, high school is known for being *the* time for gossiping and backstabbing. But that wasn't the case. The program was so beneficial, so special, so important for us, and the confidentiality was sacred. We were peers who supported one another, as opposed to peers who merely existed in the same space and time. A group of strangers became a group of friends who shared common experiences and feelings. All of a sudden, high school, a place that had seemed so huge and scary, became much smaller and more supportive. People I never thought I'd have anything in common with became an incredible part of my journey in those three years. They were shoulders to cry on, faces to smile at, and laughs to accompany mine. Venting and spilling our innermost secrets and fears allowed us to let go of so much negative emotion. It wasn't about giving someone advice; it was about listening so you could ask insightful questions and allow them to come up with their own solutions. That simple act, and having them do the same for you, became a powerful, impactful gift—one that will stay with me the rest of my life.

To this day, I cherish what I learned through Peer Support and love running into fellow group members and reminiscing about our time together. The program not only gave me a sense of belonging, but also the certainty that sharing my story doesn't have to be so scary. Speaking our minds and letting others in is a crucial step in self-reflection, in figuring out who we are and navigating the murky waters of growing up.

Because of how much Peer Support meant to me, I decided to dedicate myself to that kind of outreach and to join organizations with a similar mission. My mom served on the board of a local counseling center in Beverly Hills and, after years of witnessing her involvement, I too joined as their youngest member. During my time there, I helped raise money and establish a program whose mission was the same as Peer Support's: connecting group members simply through the act of talking. There, however, the groups included kids and parents (family members were split into different groups to avoid awkwardness). By involving both generations in the conversation, the hope was that a parent could learn something new from a child their own child's age, and vice versa. We aimed to bridge the gap between generations and promote conversation at home as a means for growing and understanding each other better. By sharing, we learn that we're not alone and that we're not so different after all. We can make a difference not only to those close to us, but to those we never even knew.

I believe that this kind of impact can happen in small groups or among crowds of thousands, which is why I've gotten involved in an event called We Day. We Days celebrate youth who are giving back to their communities and promoting empowerment across the world. It's been such an honor to speak to these huge crowds—once, it was 18,000 people!—who are dedicated to spreading love and acceptance and making a difference.

THE COLLINS LADIES REPRESENTING BYSTANDER REVOLUTION AT WE DAY.

I've had the pleasure of meeting many brave, inspiring kids who stand up against bullying, encourage the understanding and acceptance of our differences, and speak out about issues affecting all of us. They are the proof that all of our stories matter. They are the proof that sharing our stories is key. It doesn't matter where we're from, what we look like, how old we are, or who we love—we all deserve to talk and connect. We all deserve to feel part of something greater. Because we are.

The more characters you meet, the more character you build. The more colorful your story, the more colorful your life.

FROM PEN TO PAPER AND BEYOND

Storytelling is one of the most universal tools we can use to relate to one another. Through stories we convey emotions, communicate ideas, and connect with people all over the world. We can tell our stories by writing them down in journals for our own reflection; putting words in a book, screenplay, or social media post; or speaking publicly to a crowd or in front of a camera. But no matter *how* we choose to do it, the important thing is that we open up and share. I know it's easier said than done—writing this book has been an incredible lesson in that. Letting people in is difficult. We're afraid of being vulnerable, feeling judged, or appearing weak. However, it's through using our voices, both written and spoken, that we become stronger.

Storytelling allows us to make connections and start conversations in which we learn we're never alone.

Engaging others through storytelling is a real gift, one that my dad definitely has. When I was little, he used to read to me before I went to bed. It didn't matter if I'd heard the same story every single night for days. When he did all the different voices, the book came alive in a whole new way each night.

And not many people know this, but he was actually an actor before he was a musician. He performed on stage growing up, playing the Artful Dodger in *Oliver!* on the West End, and then acted in a number of films and on TV as an adult. So it's not surprising that I enjoy telling stories just as he does. It's in my blood. And like him, I wanted to share my passions with others, both through acting and through writing. It was my dad's bravery in putting himself out there in his music and lyrics that partially inspired me. Putting pen to paper has proved to be such a fulfilling outlet for me, which was one of the main reasons I got into journalism at fifteen. I was sitting with my mom at our kitchen table in the English countryside one summer flipping through my favorite magazines when I thought, why on earth was there never anything written by someone my age? All the articles were geared toward young girls, but were always from an older perspective. The writers' recommendations about what they *thought* girls would like were good, but I wanted to read something by someone who *knew*, someone who had a younger voice and point of view.

Mom and I began brainstorming ideas, and I found some phone numbers at the back of each magazine. One by one, I cold-called and asked to speak with editors. I had nothing to lose and everything to gain. I was just a girl with an idea and the drive to pursue it. Some magazines never answered, others hung up on me, and two put me through to someone in charge. One kind of liked the idea but didn't have the space or time to hear more. The other editor, at *Elle Girl* UK, was very intrigued and asked to see writing samples and meet with me as soon as possible. I couldn't believe it! Not only had I been successful in booking a meeting, now I had to come up with mock-ups of my vision. I didn't have anything but school papers on my computer, and no internet connection to send them with. So I got creative and drafted a proposal, which I had to email from an internet cafe miles away, and I printed out photos and old essays to put in a portfolio I'd immediately gone out and bought. Then I picked out a cute yet professional outfit and jumped on the train to London. I made my mom sit outside the office while I went in and pitched my concept of what would later become a feature called "LA Confidential." It would cover the latest hot spots, buzzwords, activities, and places to see in Los Angeles, complete with personal photos. The goal was simple: write a monthly article geared toward girls in the UK about what life was like in LA. I wanted it to be relatable no matter whether they lived in a big city like London or in the countryside where I was from. When Claire, my soon-to-be editor, gave me the job on the spot, I was speechless. I had actually gone out and made something happen based only on passion and an idea.

LA Confidential

New correspondent Lily Collins reports from
Beverly Hills on the latest trends to hit Hollywood

#1 Flea-market finds, Stateside

'Hey!' Over here in the States, we ELLEgirls always want to know about life in the UK – and from your letters to the team at *ELLEgirl* UK, it seems you want to know as much about the US. So here goes – this is the first of my monthly reports on new styles, the places to go and updates on what I've been doing, to give you a feel for life as an ELLEgirl on the other side of the Pond.

'But before I get started, let me tell you a little about myself... I was actually born in Guildford, Surrey, so technically I'm a Brit, but my mom and I moved here when I was six. I'll be 16 in March and eligible for my long-awaited driving licence. I'm an aspiring actress/singer and live in the heart of celeb-crowded Beverly Hills. Life over here can be surreal and exciting, but

'FOR A TREAT I HEAD TO THE ROSE BOWL'

underneath all that glamour, it's basically the same – American ELLEgirls are as on the ball, style savvy and SUSSED as they are in the UK!

'My friends and I have recently picked up on the vintage vibe, hitting local flea markets for the best fashion finds. This month I've been to two of the hottest. The Melrose Trading Post flea market at Fairfax High School, which is low-key with a lively atmosphere, is held each Sunday and opens at 10am, and I go whenever I can for an hour or two.

'But for a real treat, I head to the Rose Bowl flea market at 1001 Rose Bowl Drive, Pasadena,

which is on the second Sunday of each month. Due to its early start (ugh!), a stop at Starbucks is a necessity. Armed with an iced chai tea latte and muffin, I head for the vintage clothing and accessories stalls.

'The great thing about flea markets is that they're a social occasion too. Even though Rose Bowl is huge, I always run into people I know. I recently went with a friend and we came back with bags filled with glam gear. I found vintage Lacoste sweaters, cowboy boots, belts, purses and, of course, tons of jewellery. Our motto is: "Better to buy vintage than to spend much more for a brand-name item." You don't have to be a model or a celeb and pay haute couture prices to work the latest runway trend – we do it every day, and most of our styles originate from these flea markets!'

this month I've been mainly...

SHOPPING: My best buys this month are – you guessed it, vintage – cute pins, badges and dresses. The older the piece, you can bet how much more valuable and unique it will be.

EXERCISING: All my friends and I are really into working out – it's a very LA thing! We always make it a social gathering and have a good gossip while we're toning our bods. Pilates is my new fave class I felt really into the first time I tried it, but I reckon it's gonna be a winner for really toning up and feeling good about myself.

GIGGING: I recently went to see a gig by my friend's band Brixton at the Whisky on the Sunset Strip in West Hollywood. This place has been rocking since 1964 and is an way cool. The Doors, Janis Joplin and Led Zeppelin have all played there. Undiscovered bands play nightly and well-known artists often make appearances too. Check it out at www.whiskyagogo.com

WATCHING: The new season of The O.C. has just started in LA. We at last, the best show in the world is finally back and I have to tell you, it's hotter than ever!

SLEEPING: I'm loving 'Berry Fulfilling', a healthy fruit-and-ice-drink from our local branch at smoothies store Jamba Juice.

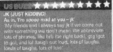
From there I found myself completely inspired. I felt driven to connect with girls my age all across the world. I was proof that it's possible to have lots in common with other people no matter

where you live. I started getting letters from readers expressing how much they liked my articles and how some had even visited the places I'd written about. This feedback inspired my editor to ask me to start writing editorials but, just after I was presented with this opportunity, *Elle Girl* folded. Luckily, when Claire left, she took me with her to her next job where I wrote a few pieces. I also started doing freelance work for *CosmoGirl* in the US and wrote Scarlett Johansson's November 2008 cover feature on the importance of voting, as well as online pieces for *Teen Vogue* and *Seventeen*. I was even made a contributing editor for the *Los Angeles Times Magazine* (where I got my first official business cards)! I felt like a legitimate journalist who was not only telling her own stories but breaking newsworthy ones as well.

The more I wrote, the more I found in common with my readers. I used my writing as a real form of self-expression, as a place to share my ideas, perspective, and voice. I also now had a platform to give others a voice. I could ask the questions I knew people my age wanted to ask but were afraid to or didn't know how to. Through me, young readers could become educated on certain topics or discover new perspectives on fashion, politics, entertainment, family, self-esteem, and all those lovely things every young woman faces. No topic was off-limits or too awkward. And if that meant me admitting something embarrassing to start off the conversation, then so be it!

After finding my voice in journalism, I decided I wanted to use it to reach even more people. And the most logical medium for that was TV. I was driven by the same belief as before: a younger voice representing the younger generation can make a huge difference. There was something much more relatable about a teenager telling the stories, asking the questions, and reporting back. So I pitched talk show ideas to networks, and started working for Nickelodeon. I began by hosting a summer show called *Slime Across America* (yes, I experienced that childhood dream of being slimed, and apart from being hot, sticky, and smelling slightly disgusting, it felt amazing). As that job was coming to an end, I spoke with the network about staying on and reporting for them full time. I started hosting little segments in between their normal programming and doing pieces on red carpets at film premieres, working my way up to reporting live from the orange carpet at the Kids' Choice Awards.

PSYCHED TO BE SLIMED! MY OFFICIAL BACKSTAGE PRESS PASS
FOR THE NICKELODEON KIDS' CHOICE AWARD'S ORANGE CARPET.

I also took part in their Kids Pick the President campaign during the 2008 election. As an eighteen-year-old college student, I traveled to the Democratic and Republican conventions asking voters, delegates, and other campaign professionals about the key topics being discussed by the candidates and what I should know as a first-time voter. I even got to report from President Obama's inauguration in Washington! It was freezing and I could barely move my lips but I witnessed history being made. It was an incredible learning experience to take part in something so important and do it in a way that was not only exciting but also relatable to young people. By using *my* voice I was able to give a voice to an entire audience and generation.

THE BIG DAY! ON LOCATION IN WASHINGTON FOR NICKELODEON'S KIDS PICK THE PRESIDENT CAMPAIGN 2008.

It's not just in the act of telling stories that we see their greatest impact. It's in the aftermath, in the conversations they promote and inspire. We blindly put ourselves out there, hoping to make a connection but not knowing for sure if we will. That's exactly what your favorite author, journalist, actor, or musician does every day. What compels you to pay attention to their words? What is it about their stories that makes you feel connected to them? Now think about how powerful that book, article, movie, or album is if it makes people all over the world feel just as affected as you do. Those stories teach us, unite us, inspire us. Their *authors* inspire us. And, who knows, you too may already serve as a huge inspiration for someone. So keep using your voice, honoring your past, owning your story, and making new experiences to add to it. The more characters you meet, the more character you build. The more colorful your story, the more colorful your life.

Our greatest triumphs in life don't come without having to navigate both the ups and the downs.

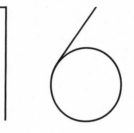

EVERYTHING HAPPENS FOR A REASON

' ve always believed that there are two ways to accept being told no: You hear "No, this isn't for you," or you hear "No, this isn't for you *right now.*" Either you accept defeat, letting someone else dictate how you live your life and whether you're up to a challenge. Or you accept the current situation for what it is and figure out a way to turn that no right now into a yes later. Perhaps a few other things just need to fall into place first! How you handle the next phase of your life, your next set of experiences, all those obstacles the world throws your way in the meantime—that defines who you are and what you really want. Because that frustrating roadblock might open you up to something even better down the road. Which is exactly what I think about to stay motivated and keep up my positive attitude, even in the most heartbreaking of circumstances.

Let's rewind. When I was sixteen, I wanted to be the youngest talk show host ever, a mix of Tyra Banks, Ellen DeGeneres, and Barbara Walters. Quite a combo, right? Just as I believed that magazines targeting young people needed young voices, I believed there was also a hole on television with how my age demographic was represented. I did the research to prove it, making bar graphs and charts and creating an entire presentation. I had two very different concepts for a show: one idea was to have a panel of young people, including yours truly, discuss current events and topics, and then we'd interview a celebrity guest plus a non-celebrity expert from a specific field, much like *The View*; the other idea was for me to interview celebrities, meeting them wherever they felt most comfortable or going somewhere they loved and doing an activity together, like cooking at their home, playing games at an amusement park, going on a hike, or painting at a studio—whatever made them tick. I thought both concepts would have a younger, more modern flavor than traditional shows.

So there I was, sixteen-year-old Lily, armed with a thousand printouts and ready to kill it. I went into boardroom after boardroom of network executives forty years older than I was. Most of them simply stared, treating me like some silly little girl pitching huge ideas. They questioned my audience, convinced that no one could relate to someone so young. (This was, after all, long before YouTube, Twitter, Instagram, etc. became popular.) They didn't understand what my intention was or acknowledge that young people needed a voice—*wanted* a voice. I was told no more times than I can remember. So even though I had a clear vision, a plan of attack, and the eagerness to take on the challenge, I ultimately couldn't convince them to take the risk and buy into either concept.

REPORTING FOR DUTY: COVERING THE 2008
PRESIDENTIAL CAMPAIGN FOR NICKELODEON!

This is where my everything-happens-for-a-reason mantra makes all the difference: the way I see it, if things back then had worked out how I wanted, I wouldn't be where I am now as an actor. But that realization didn't come easy. It took a little time, some self-doubt, and a lot of frustration to get there. After I landed my first couple of acting jobs, I was able to look back and acknowledge that I wouldn't have gone down this path if the other one had been clear. Because the more an audience saw "real Lily" on a talk show as a TV personality, the harder it would have been for them to believe me as characters in films or shows. Which is why, heartwrenching as it was, being told no in that situation was a blessing in disguise.

At the same time I was trying to launch the talk show—because apparently I could never focus on one thing at a time!—I was also exploring modeling and acting, two fields full of rejection. I've gone in for plenty of castings where I heard no before I even walked in the door. I remember being devastated when I lost out on an Abercrombie & Fitch campaign and when I didn't look old enough for a perfume ad. Over the years I've been turned down because I looked too young, too old, didn't have the right hair color, wasn't experienced enough, or just plain and simple wasn't what they had in mind. And each job I didn't get felt like a failure. I'll never forget the day I found out I wouldn't be playing Jenny Humphrey on *Gossip Girl* and living out my NYC dream. I doubted myself a lot in those situations. But instead of believing that I wasn't good enough and getting discouraged, I tried my best to take criticism and learn and grow from it. And often it wasn't until another amazing script or opportunity arose that I could completely put it into perspective and realize it was all happening for a reason. And with modeling, after coming to terms with my body issues and eating disorders, I'm quite thankful that career didn't take off. It wasn't a healthy environment for me after all, and I think the universe was telling me that in its own way.

(LILY) COLLINS PLAYING COLLINS (TUOHY)
ON SET FOR *THE BLIND SIDE*.

As I got older and life got more complicated, fate definitely didn't stop making things difficult. I remember facing college applications and waiting anxiously for acceptances to come in the mail. Certain envelopes delivered great news, and those that didn't made your heart drop as you felt the weight of rejection. Or you'd get into two schools you were excited about and didn't know which was best for you. So many people give you their (unsolicited) opinions, it can seem like yours gets lost along the way! I applied to quite a few schools, didn't get into some, but received acceptances at two that I was really proud of: USC in California and NYU in New York. As much as I wanted to move away from home, I also knew LA was where I needed to be for work. I had spent so much time and energy pursuing what I loved that it would be a step backward for me to leave. So I decided to stay home and continue pursuing acting outside of classes and see what happened.

OFFICIAL COLLEGE STUDENT! TOURING THE USC CAMPUS
DURING ORIENTATION FRESHMAN YEAR.

And then, after all that agonizing, ultimately I ended up having to leave school at the end of my sophomore year anyway. There came a point, after traveling back and forth across the US while shooting *The Blind Side* in Atlanta, when I couldn't balance it all anymore. At first I gave myself a hard time. But I realized that I didn't want to live with any regrets, and I knew I'd regret not taking advantage of the career opportunities in front of me. One day, if I wanted to, I'd go back and really commit the time and get my degree in something I was super interested in. My guidance counselor talked me through the entire thing and was really supportive. If I hadn't chosen USC, I may not have had that same encouragement and help to make the transition.

The question of "Why is this happening?" is hard when dealing with career stuff and hard with school stuff, too. But it's positively gut-wrenching when it comes to dating. You can spend so much time and energy questioning yourself—what went wrong, who's to blame, could I have done something differently—that it can prevent you from moving on. I think every breakup is a journey of realizing that the universe has something greater in mind for you. Trust me, I get it: ending a relationship feels like the end of the world. Sometimes it felt like I'd never be happy again. But as time passes and your heart mends, you pick yourself up and carry on. And at least now you know what your heart is capable of feeling. I always had to believe that this one person was meant to teach me something about myself to get me ready for whoever was coming my way next. Admittedly, it wouldn't be until I met that next person—who brought out in me the new things I'd learned or parts of myself I'd gotten in touch with—that faith was truly restored. Like the time I fell for this slightly older guy who was the first guy ever to tell me directly that he wasn't ready for a relationship. The intense heartbreak was the absolute worst, but the clarity and honesty of the situation helped me move forward without any confusion. Then, a couple years later when I found myself in his shoes—a place no one enjoys being—I knew how to properly address the situation rather than string my then-boyfriend along.

Sometimes, though, the *reason* part of "everything happens for a reason" is harder to see. We wonder what we did to deserve so much pain; we wonder what the point of it all is. But finding some kind of deeper meaning is the only way to bring light to the darkest times in our lives. For instance, if I hadn't been in my emotionally abusive relationship, I may never have found my voice and figured out how to stand up to him and others like him in the future. I always try to do that kind of reframing with every type of relationship that doesn't work out. I never like referring to them as "failed" because I learn so much from each one, gaining a better sense of who I am and what I need, and what I can give to someone else. It can take knowing what you don't want or shouldn't ever put up with to value someone who treats you amazingly and to appreciate what it feels like to be the best version of yourself with another person. I truly believe we all have the power to take situations into our own hands, but I also know that believing in the power of fate allows me to be more at peace when something ends, because I can see it as a new beginning.

Our greatest triumphs in life don't come without having to navigate the ups *and* the downs. I, for one, wouldn't be as proud of what I've done if I hadn't worked so hard to accomplish it. And at the end of the day, believing that everything happens for a reason takes a huge weight off my shoulders. I still face opposition constantly, but it only makes me fight harder. It gives me perspective and reminds me that I can't control anything except for the way I handle myself in each situation and how I move forward and accept the cards I've been dealt. So, thank you to all those people who have dealt me a crappy hand and told me no—it's made hearing yes that much better.

The universe gives us nuggets of inspiration every once in a while during our most trying times and, if we're open and willing to see, they can prompt immense growth.

SEOUL SEARCHING

'm in the middle of filming a movie in South Korea, and I find myself sitting alone at the same table at my hotel for hours every day, drinking tea and overlooking Seoul. And despite being one of ten million people in this city right now, there are moments of utter loneliness. I am homesick. I feel simultaneously separate from and completely immersed in this incredible place. I've done my best to get out and explore the city when I'm not working, finding local hot spots and hidden gems. But feeling homesick and playing tourist are no excuse—I need to buckle down and finish writing this book. I'd rather keep procrastinating because it feels like the only way to keep my story open, the only way to edit and rewrite and never submit my final draft. I just have no idea how I'm supposed to wrap all this up, how I'm supposed to write my own ending.

I remember when I first started conceptualizing *Unfiltered* and figuring out which stories and experiences to share—the journey ahead seemed impossible. I had never been so raw and honest before. I had never shared so many parts of myself. But I knew that if I could open up, not only would I help others to do the same, *I* would come out the other side stronger. And it was true: the more I wrote and got off my chest, the more I opened up to people in every part of my life. If someone raised an awkward or taboo subject I could relate to, I'd join the conversation. I found myself being unfiltered. Speaking without boundaries, without walls. And the more I spoke, the more I engaged with others who had similar stories. I was in the position I hoped my future readers would be one day: not feeling different, crazy, or alone. Feeling supported. Revealing my secrets and experiences turned into a kind of therapy. One I hadn't even known I needed. It made me realize that my life was never going to be perfect. It's an ever-evolving story, one that has ebbs and flows, lightness and darkness, with new chapters constantly being added when I least expect it. The universe gives us nuggets of inspiration every once in a while during our most trying times and, if we're open and willing to see, they can provide us with immense growth. And that's exactly what happened during my time in Korea.

ME IN A NUTSHELL EVERY DAY IN SEOUL, AT A
CORNER TABLE WITH MY COMPUTER, GOING SLIGHTLY CRAZY.

But before diving into Korea, I need to back up first and explain the situation leading up to it. I had flown straight to Seoul after shooting an extremely emotional and incredibly moving film, *To the Bone*, which was one of the most terrifying and beautiful experiences I've ever had. Like me, my character, Ellen, battles with eating disorders, and when I was first considering the role, the thought of stepping back into those shoes made my stomach drop. I would need to lose a significant amount of weight and, even though it would be for a specific purpose and under the strict supervision of a nutritionist, I was nervous about the regimented diet, the self-discipline, and the psychological effects. Not to mention that, in order to accurately portray the disease and

Ellen's mental state, I'd need to tap back into my old, unhealthy mindset. Would I be able to truly separate myself from the role and keep from undoing all the progress I'd made? I didn't want old triggers to get the best of me or to get caught up in it all again. Sure, I was ten years past the height of my eating issues, but you really never stop being in recovery. It's a constant process. Still, deep in my heart, I knew that I had to go through it. I couldn't turn down an opportunity like that, one that would force me to confront my past issues and be recorded on film forever. It was important for me and for anyone who needs to hear a story like this, one that pulls back the curtain on a topic still considered taboo despite growing more common among males and females of all ages. And I can't tell you how glad I am I did the movie. It was beyond empowering to face the disorder head-on and erase all shame surrounding it. And taking part in such a brave and public endeavor was also very in line with my book. If I hadn't been writing and pouring my heart out already, I don't know if I would have said yes to the film. I certainly wouldn't have been able to be as exposed in my performance. Until I wrote my chapters about food and eating disorders, which I coincidentally finished a week before reading the *To the Bone* script, I hadn't yet been completely honest with myself about the past and what had happened.

In the end, *To the Bone* turned out to be the best form of creative rehab, helping me face aspects of my disorder I'd never fully addressed. And when it was over, I found myself in a remission period where I felt stronger than I had ten years ago at the height of my disorder, but also still vulnerable. The physical and emotional effects of the experience I'd just had were still so fresh. I was, however, determined to stay focused on my growth rather than dwelling on any signs of potential weakness—I only had about a week to breathe before I was off to start filming in Korea for *Okja*. I had to travel across the world, totally alone, to an extremely foreign country. And in this new film, I was playing a physically strong young woman who is tasked with protecting those weaker than herself. Worlds apart from what I'd just shot! Literally and figuratively. I had to put the *To the Bone* weight back on in a healthy way, not only for me to regain strength as Lily, but also to inhabit the mind of my badass character, who had zero connection to disordered eating. I would look at my very thin body in the hotel-room mirror and think about how, ten years ago, this was all I'd wanted, to be that skinny. It would have been my dream. And it would have been easy for my mind to trick me into thinking it still was. But that was the past. I wasn't that girl anymore. And so I found myself living a metaphor: leaving my old ways and old body behind and becoming the strong person I wanted to be. I saw it as the universe giving me the best excuse to get healthy again and not dwell in the mindset of sickness, something Lily-ten-years-ago would totally have done. It meant finally opening doors within myself that had been closed for years.

But unlocking these doors forced me to confront memories

and emotions I'd tried to suppress or assumed I'd gotten over. There were moments in Korea when I thought I might fail, might regress. I was afraid I'd get sucked back into the disorder and deviate from my road to health. I was in a country where I barely understood what anyone was saying and hardly recognized most of the food. A good friend of mine had said it would be much harder gaining back the weight than losing it—and she'd been right. But I made a conscious effort not to let my old fears get the best of me. I'd fought too hard to let them win now. I sat with my thoughts and let them be there. I spoke to my mom and my friends when I was feeling weak and alone. I welcomed any and all guidance with open arms, and sought the love and support of those closest to me. I knew that I needed them and that it was okay. They were incredibly supportive, not afraid to speak bluntly and honestly. One of my girlfriends urged me not to be hard on myself and not to be afraid of letting go. I needed to view my focus as getting *me* back, not as gaining weight back. And although it would take me longer than anticipated, eventually I would do it. I would get healthy again. I would recover my strength.

Struggling is normal. It's human. But I didn't let my new struggles define me. I used them for deep self-reflection and emotional contemplation. I filled myself up with food that was fulfilling and that gave me the fuel I needed to think, explore, and write. I reincorporated new food groups and even had some pork and beef for the first time in fifteen years at an amazing Korean

BBQ joint. I also had the incredible opportunity to cook with the renowned and revered Buddhist monk Chef Jeong Kwan.

THE ARRAY OF EXQUISITE DISHES WE PREPARED WITH
CHEF JEONG KWAN, INCLUDING CLASSIC KOREAN KIMCHI,
GREEN ONION PANCAKES, SALADS, AND SAUCES.

I continued my culinary exploration when I returned to LA after filming. All of a sudden lunches and dinners lasted hours as I tried new things, shared plates, even ordered dessert while chatting with friends, just enjoying their company and allowing the act of eating to be a fun social event. I found that I didn't need to carry around and rely on my staple food supplies, and didn't need to panic if I didn't know what or where I would eat next. I also began to exercise again. But instead of going full speed ahead and burning out, I took my time and set my own pace. I didn't feel guilty about not working out every single day. I reintroduced myself to my body and listened to its needs, giving it a rest when it needed one. I embraced change and learned that there is such a thing as healthy control. I am the key to my own healing. In order to get healthy, I needed to take action because I *wanted* to. Whatever muscle or weight my body acquired from here on out would be because of hard work, sweat, and love. It would come from a positive and nurturing place of pride. Maybe I would finally be able to see what my normal, natural body was. I accepted the organic progression of things; if I felt full, perhaps more than I would have once felt comfortable with, I sat with my discomfort and pushed away those familiar feelings of guilt. Then shockingly, three hours later, I felt better, sometimes even hungry again. After restricting my body for years and not letting it respond naturally to what it needed, allowing this progression of digestion and feeling what my body required was incredible. I felt fulfilled in all ways as I immersed myself in this educational and therapeutic experience. A true mind, body, soul connection.

SENSORY OVERLOAD IN GWANGJANG MARKET.

Then something unexpected happened. Through all this healing and self-reflection, I came to meet the voice of my own addiction. I'd listened to those of my addict exes but never knew that *I* had one myself—and that it was *loud*. It had been controlling, too, telling me what to do and influencing my actions. That was terrifying. The more work I did on myself, the more I was able to separate the addiction's voice from the true voice inside me. And now that I've turned up the volume on my own voice, and turned down that of my addiction, it's helped me understand the importance of finding a healthy balance. The more I think about the future, the more certain I am that I don't want to carry my emotional baggage with me anymore. I'm twenty-seven, and one day I want a family. I want kids. I know it's part of my greater purpose. I want to live for someone more than just myself and, when I do, I want to be the happiest and healthiest I can be. I don't want to pass down my issues to my kids. Instead, I want to pass down stories. I want to be one of those people who remembers the random, beautiful details about even the most fleeting moments in life. I want to look back and know I didn't waste a moment sweating the small stuff, didn't allow anything or anyone to dim my light. I want to look as strong as I feel. And in order to do all of that, I need to live my life for every moment and be truly present, not worried about things that are out of my control or trying to control everything within my power.

In the end, I refuse to let this role I've become so accustomed to playing in my daily life—Girl with a Disorder—define who I am today and who I become. I know that losing that title scares part of me; I also know that I'm more than just my body. I don't need to label myself. None of us do. I remember driving home the night we wrapped filming on *To the Bone* and passing my high school where many of my insecurities, relationship problems, and eating issues had begun. I looked out the window and smiled. Little did I know that the troubled Lily back then was going through it all for a greater purpose. To be able to one day share her story as part of a much larger one. To have her voice join the voices of so many other young women. And I can't tell you how freeing it is to share and be open. To be transparent. It's a weight off my shoulders, a self-inflicted burden relinquished. I have so many other things to focus on, moments to look forward to, and I've found comfort in knowing that treatment is forever. I don't have a time limit or deadline before I have to figure it all out. There is no end point, only progress. And I'm making it in steps both big and small. I want to know who I am underneath all those layers I built over the years. Sometimes it takes revisiting our past to prepare for our future. I know this has always sounded incredibly cheesy to me, but it's true now more than ever: I'm not getting any younger, and the sooner I accept my story for all that it is, and let go of the shame, regrets, and fear surrounding my experiences, the sooner I can just live, love, and be loved.

Being healthy no longer
equaled looking perfect.
Instead, it represented how
strong I felt inside.

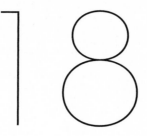

DARING TO BARE

This time around, writing a new chapter is a very different story. Well, maybe not so much a *different story*, but definitely a different situation. I'm in a different state physically and a different place emotionally. Which is exactly why I wanted to write a little more for the paperback version of *Unfiltered*, to add a sort of status update. As I was racking my brain trying to come up with the perfect topic for this eighteenth chapter—my lucky number, coincidentally—I started thinking about all the things that have happened since the book was first published, all the ways that I've been validated that I did the right thing by coming clean, shedding my skin, and opening up. And then it dawned on me: *that's* what I should write about. So much has changed since

I was *Seoul Searching* in my final chapter. I've learned a great deal and evolved in ways I couldn't have anticipated. It would be far too long-winded to touch on everything that's transpired, but there are a few particularly pivotal and poignant things to share, a couple new moments when I've dared to bare.

MY INCREDIBLE BOOK SIGNING IN LA! A DAY I'LL NEVER FORGET!

When I finished writing *Unfiltered* in 2016, I had just wrapped filming on *Okja* and was off to shoot another film, *Halo of Stars*, before starting press for *Rules Don't Apply*. As you can imagine, it was busy and stressful. Not only because of all the work, but also because I had a ways to go to return to the healthy weight I'd been before filming *To the Bone*. As much as

I explained to people that it was going to be a long process, they were concerned nonetheless when it appeared as though it wasn't happening fast enough. And while I expected it from my mom and my friends, I did not expect it from people in the industry. I never could have predicted the hesitation that came from casting directors and magazine editors. I didn't think they'd react so negatively to my drastic change in appearance, be so reluctant to cast me, or be so worried to show my body to their viewers and readers. And even though they knew my weight had been for a role, a number of editors came forward to share their concern. They refused to promote an unhealthy body image and, therefore, didn't want to put me in their magazines. Although I now applaud their stance on the matter and agree it was the right thing to do, at the time I was upset and frustrated. I couldn't believe how I looked was affecting my work at such a crucial time in my career. My physical appearance was restricting me from doing what I enjoyed and was holding me back from succeeding. I was determined to make the change I needed right away.

Although I had already been working extremely hard with my nutritionist and trainer to gain more muscle mass and add definition back to my frame, I had to amp it up and start treating the process like a job. My progress had to move more quickly and I needed to stop prolonging it. Truth be told, I wasn't completely comfortable with the idea of gaining weight on purpose.

Deep-rooted uncertainty was holding me back from fully diving in and committing. But in my heart I knew I needed to practice what I was preaching. A lightbulb finally went off in my head and I knew enough was enough. All of a sudden I found myself wishing something I never would have expected: that I could gain weight with the snap of my fingers. It was the exact opposite of what I'd wanted back when my eating disorders started. But my priorities had shifted. My dreams were within reach and I wasn't about to let anything block me from them. Nevertheless, as much as I wished it were as easy as a snap, it wasn't. And I knew I had a long road ahead of me.

That long road was absolutely worth it. Six months later, I found myself in another press-heavy schedule, gearing up to promote *Okja* and *To the Bone*, which were coming out within a couple weeks of each other. Yet again I was faced with doing potential magazine shoots—one of which, ironically, ended up taking place at Vasquez Rocks, the desert location in California where I had filmed the ending of *To the Bone*. This time, being there was completely different. Things had changed; I had changed. I was no longer portraying a physically weak and insecure young woman on the brink of death. I was living the life of a strong, healthy woman ready to take on the world. Not only had I gained weight back, I, more importantly, felt stronger and healthier than ever. My hard work was paying off. So much so that I even booked the cover of *Shape* magazine! What?! Yes, I was going to be featured on the cover of a women's fitness and wellness magazine whose very name represents something I used to shy away from, used to fear. Furthermore, I was going to be on the cover of their summer issue, the biggest of the year, in only a bathing suit! Excuse me?! Yet again, something I never thought I'd do, considering I used to avoid wearing bathing suits in public as much as possible. They represented a form of torture, the ultimate breeding ground for my insecurities. But now, I was totally game and ready to stand proudly and bare all. Well, not exactly ALL . . . but a heck of a lot more skin than I'd ever felt comfortable sharing before.

ME CELEBRATING MY JOURNEY ON VASQUEZ ROCKS.

Gearing up for the *Shape* shoot was nerve-racking. But instead of driving myself crazy to look "perfect," I continued to focus on feeling stronger and more confident. And boy did I! That day was something I'll never forget. Not just because it was incredibly cold and windy and I was wearing next to nothing, but because I was able to stand tall and embrace my body as it was without feeling insecure. I enjoyed the experience and felt beautiful. I was so proud of how far I'd come and of the new normal I'd become accustomed to within my own skin. Even if I found myself thinking about how I looked and feeling nervous, I never showed it. I didn't let insecurity win. I knew that if I didn't put it out there, it wouldn't have any power over me. I could control how much I allowed my insecurities to dictate my happiness. Being healthy no longer equaled looking perfect. Instead, it represented how strong I felt inside. And that day, I felt super strong. Shooting that specific cover meant more to me than shooting a normal fashion spread. It represented so much more. It signified change, growth, and progress. To think that only half a year before I was told I couldn't even appear within the inside pages of some fashion magazines. . . .

SOAKING UP THE SUN AND FEELING FREE WHILE SHOOTING
FOR *SHAPE* MAGAZINE!

I was not only in a different physical state than when I originally finished writing this book, but also a different emotional
one. I had only just admitted a lot of the things I wrote about
to myself, and now I was on the brink of admitting them to the
world, of putting it all out there. It's pretty appropriate, then,
that right after this book landed on shelves, I attended my ten-
year high school reunion. Yup, that's right. High school. THE
time and place when a lot of the struggles I discuss in the book
materialized.

I have no idea how on earth it's even possible that I had

graduated ten years ago! The time seems to have completely flown by and I don't feel nearly old enough.

I've driven by Harvard-Westlake countless times since I graduated but have seldom gone inside to visit. I've always seen those gates as welcoming but also quite daunting. Needless to say, when I found out that there was going to be a proper celebration for the occasion, I was filled with mixed emotions. Of course, I wanted to go but, at the same time, I was nervous to face a crowd that was now privy to so many personal admissions about my time there. Ultimately, I knew I couldn't skip it. After all, you only get one first high school reunion. Thankfully my closest friends from school were also attending and we all decided to go together. The drive there was a combination of amping ourselves up and calming our nerves. As excited as I was, I was also apprehensive because I hadn't kept up with what everyone had been doing. Heck, I wasn't even expecting to recognize everyone! But the main reason I was nervous was because the beginning of these ten years also marked the height of my eating disorder. It represented the time when I was struggling the most. It was also the period of my life when I was hiding and lying, mostly to myself but also to everyone else. I didn't know if I'd face backlash or negativity from old friends; I wasn't sure if the kids who had suspected my issues would say "I told you so." I knew that some level of nerves was normal and expected, but I couldn't help feeling they were amplified because the reunion coincided with the release of my book. Then again, as a firm believer in "everything happens for a reason," I wasn't *that* surprised.

BEING BACK THERE FELT LIKE NO TIME HAD GONE BY AT ALL! IT WAS SO SURREAL TO BE BACK A DECADE LATER WITH A HEALTHY MINDSET, FRESH PERSPECTIVE, AND ABSOLUTE EMOTIONAL FREEDOM.

As my friends and I walked into school, we grabbed hands and promised that it was going to be a fun, positive experience. Little did I know just how fun, positive, and meaningful it would be!

Stepping onto that campus and into those classrooms flooded me with memories. We all immediately reverted back to being rowdy teenagers and it really was amazing to see those

I hadn't seen in ages. My apprehension about the book and people's potential reactions was squashed almost as soon as I got there. All I could see were friendly faces and everyone's shared enthusiasm for being there. I wasn't singled out or condemned. Instead, some of my old peers even came up to congratulate and commend me on being so vocal. One classmate, who had been in my Peer Support group when I was a group leader, recalled a day we were hanging out after school talking about all the pressures we had been feeling. He recounted specific things I had said about my body image issues, work, and family that I don't even remember revealing. He then revealed to me what he had been going through at that time. As I sat there listening, it dawned on me that although I'd suspected that he'd been dealing with a lot too, I never knew to what extent. I realized that behind closed doors, those secret struggles must have existed for every single person in Peer Support. For every person in my entire class. He echoed that thought when he said to me, "Come on. Everyone in this room was going through something. We were all trying to be perfect." And it's so true! We all were. Even though my story was unique, it was also one of many. And I hadn't been the only one hiding or lying. That classmate's support, and the suppprt of so many others that night, was unexpected and encouraging. I would never have thought all those years ago that I'd one day be owning up to my struggles, let alone in such a public way. I wouldn't have thought I'd be strong enough or brave enough. But I was, and it made me feel so empowered. Those ten years since graduation may not have aged me *that* much physically, but they matured me emotionally. Speaking out about my experiences allowed me to walk back into my high school with a newfound perspective and understanding. It allowed me to have closure on that chapter of my life and to move forward with a clean slate. I could finally own the struggles of my teenage self and use them to empower the woman I'd since become.

Between reminiscing about old memories and making new ones, the aftermath of publishing *Unfiltered* has been transformative. I set out to write the book so that others would feel less alone. But as it happened, it's constantly reminded me that *I'm* not alone. Every single time someone approaches me and tells me their stories or shares experiences that relate to mine, I'm reaffirmed. What a beautiful gift! I've also had some of the most intimate heart-to-heart conversations with my friends who read the book and were left with questions. It's been freeing to be such an open book (pun intended!) and to see how explaining myself frees them in return. It helps them understand me and my struggles better, as well as alleviating any guilt they feel for not having been aware or not having seen through my lies. It wasn't their fault for not knowing what I was going through.

As I wrote in chapter two, we all can do a good job of hiding—and that's exactly what I had done. In fact, I'd mastered that skill. But not anymore! Hiding is no longer even a word in my daily vocabulary. It's never gotten me anywhere positive anyway. Openness and acceptance is where I exist now. Daring myself to go outside my comfort zone and bare my body and soul—whether in an old classroom at my high school reunion or in a bathing suit at a photo shoot—is my new way of life. And let me tell you: it's working wonders so far.

MICHELLE OBAMA

April 3, 2017

Ms. Lily Collins
Los Angeles, California

Dear Lily:

I am writing to thank you for the copy of your new book. The gift was such a nice gesture and I look forward to sharing it with my daughters.

The outpouring of support I have received from women across the country continues to amaze me, and I am filled with a great sense of hope for our shared future. I heard this quote recently and it reminded me of your book so I wanted to share it with you.

"Here's to strong women, may we know them,
    may we be them, may we raise them."

Again, thank you for your kindness, Lily. I wish you all the best.

Warmly,

Michelle Obama

ONE OF THE MOST EXCITING LETTERS I HAVE EVER
GOTTEN! WHAT AN ABSOLUTE HONOR.

Love Always
and
Forever

ACKNOWLEDGMENTS

I know I've not always been the most easygoing, stress-free person, especially while writing this book, but thanks for enduring my craziness and loving me anyway. Throughout this whole journey I'm so fortunate to have been surrounded by such incredible, genuine people who have been instrumental and inspiring to my story. The following is not alphabetical or in order of importance (I promise). I love you all!

Thank you:

Mom—For being the incredible inspiration and role model that you are. For encouraging me to be so open and honest and for supporting me every step of the way through this whole journey, both with my writing process as well as in my growing up and becoming a woman. You've never judged me, only loved me. No words will ever adequately express how proud I am of you and how grateful I am for everything you've ever given me and taught me. I love you, always and forever. There's just way too much to say, so I've saved the rest for your chapter.

Dad—For always inspiring me and encouraging me to do what I love and to give it my all. Thank you for teaching me so much about myself even when you didn't know that you were. I've grown so much as a person throughout it all. I remain so proud of you for all you've done and the health changes you've bravely made. Like I've said a million times, I'll always be your little girl who will need you, no matter what, and I'm looking forward to sharing so many things to come. I love you to the moon and back again.

Thom and Bill—For never judging me and always being there for me to ask questions of. For sitting and listening all those years ago when I was struggling and didn't even know it. You imparted wisdom that I continue to pass along. You opened my eyes in ways I didn't know possible and helped me navigate my way out when I didn't see a path. Thank you for always supporting me, from my elementary school basketball games to my most recent film premieres, and for taking tons of photos to cherish forever.

Dan—For always nurturing my creative, odd, and wacky side since I was little and constantly inspiring me with your work. Your artistry never ceases to amaze me and your loving spirit is infectious.

Candice—For being the world's best nana. For always going to all the same restaurants with me out of years of habit and putting up with my complicated menu-ordering. For not rolling your eyes (at least in front of me) as I pulled out my daily yogurt and iced coffee every morning in class at USC. You knew my weird quirks back then, but embraced them as part of who I was. You never passed judgment on me and weren't afraid to speak your mind or give your opinion even when others may have filtered themselves. Thank you to your loving husband, Kyle, for also putting up with me, your other other half, and for keeping my mom company when I stole you from him.

Alex V.—For being one of the most individual and unique human beings I have the pleasure of knowing and loving. For embracing all people no matter what and for being so passionate. For sharing in my love of dressing up and going to the Renaissance Faire, for sharing your mom with me, and for loving my mom as your LA mom. Your laugh makes me smile and your hugs always make me feel better. I can't imagine where I'd be without your friendship.

Jaime and Kevin—For your constant love and support

through some of my most difficult times. I'm honored to know you and your beautiful daughters. Jaime, our priceless chats whether during take-out dinners or while getting nails done, have meant more to me than you'll ever know. I value your honest opinion and direct delivery. You never sugarcoat anything and aren't shy about voicing yourself. No matter how embarrassed other people would be, you're always so open and free. You're one of the strongest, most independent, and hilarious women I know. A breath of fresh air. Kevin, having your perspective on my guy problems has been utterly invaluable and so eye-opening. Thank you for being so honest with me and, just like your wife, never telling me what I want to hear. I honestly can't even begin to imagine surviving the past few years without you guys by my side. Your friendship is priceless. It's a joy to have been part of your journey to parenthood and to now be an honorary auntie to Zoë and Blake. You're all family and I'm always here for you no matter what.

Liana—For speaking up all those years ago when you felt something was wrong. For always being there in person or on Skype to listen to me vent or rave about boys, even when you knew they weren't good for me. For never shying away from saying so. For never keeping your mouth shut out of hesitation or fear that I wouldn't agree or like what you had to say. For visiting me on set when I was processing the aftermath of *that* awful breakup and for being exactly the medicine I needed to get my groove back. For the countless hours we've discussed our future plans and family stresses. For being there to listen to me talk through my struggles and for being my dance partner at school proms and formals as well as nights out on the town in NYC. Whether in work or play, you've always got my back and your insight has been more valuable than you know in my self-reflection process.

Mark—For encouraging me to let go and have fun. To not take life too seriously and embrace change. Also for all your unparalleled guy advice. You always seem to just get me. You never pass judgment or make me feel crazy. Unless we're being crazy together. Which I love. Your independent spirit is inspiring and you've been such a rock upon which I know I can always rely. I'll always be there for you as I know you would be for me.

Alex A.—For always being my cheerleader, for always lending a helping hand, starting in French class freshman year all the way to now when I can't figure out why technology hates me so much. For visiting me in Korea at a time when I was craving a familiar face. For bringing me snacks from home and taking me around, introducing me to people and places that made it seem less daunting. I'm so proud of all your accomplishments and the risks you take. Your support, encouragement, and patience have been a significant help to me all these years.

Lorenza—For encouraging me to embrace my sexy side. For being there to sympathize with, but also to call me out. For being patient as I continually jotted notes down during our girly venting sessions because I didn't want to forget your words of wisdom. Your humor and love of life is infectious and I couldn't be prouder of how far you've come, how much you've grown. For your incredible husband, Eli, who also let me commandeer you and steal you away for our date nights. You've been such a positive energy and source of light.

Bella—For warning me how hard this would be even though I didn't believe you. And then for still listening to my complaints and struggles when I finally understood what you meant. Thank you for introducing me to some of the most significant people in my whole journey. For all the lunches and teas and homemade meals over which we spilled secrets, bared our souls, and bonded. Your honesty and "to the point" mentality is so refreshing and I admire your ability to be selective and do only things that make you happy and feel fulfilled, never because someone else told you to.

Johnny—For being the bluntest person I know, even when it's about yourself. You've made me laugh like no other since we met in first grade all those years ago. You've not changed one bit. I rely on you to call me out and say it as it is. Thank you for never giving up on trying to convince me to eat meat and try new foods even when you're extremely persistent, bordering on annoying. I know it always comes from a place of love. Only true friends get away with that! You constantly lift me up and remind me of who I am, and always have been. Even if that's a control freak. Thank you for reminding me I'm a control freak and loving me anyway. No one has a memory like you do. Just keep some things to yourself. :) Thank you for encouraging me to dress up and make an effort. Without fail I now pull things out of my closet that I would have never worn before and I love it. You were right, it does make me feel better. And yes I know, you're still waiting for a blond moment.

Shelby—For being part of the three amigos with Johnny since the first grade. For understanding what it means to be a picky eater and take ages to order off a menu, but basically be creating your own dish. For the countless hours we've laughed together, at each other's expense. For being the incredibly fashion-savvy girl you are and inspiring me to be bolder with my style. I've come to accept that some things just look better on you. Reconnecting with you and Johnny has been so incredibly special. It's crazy how we can all just pick up right where we left off, as if no time has passed. The sign of true genuine friendship. Having your support means the world and I can't tell you how much it means to reminisce on old memories like we do every time we're together.

Carrie—For sticking by my side all these years in work and in life. For believing in me and for making others do the same. For being real, never afraid to speak up even if it's to say something you think I may not want to hear. For your unwavering support. For helping me see a way out of some dark times and having my back when it took me a little longer than I expected. You didn't give up and you made me see things in a new light. You've been more inspiring than you know. I can't imagine what I'd do without you.

Chelsea—For all our emails back and forth that make me laugh exactly when I need to. For starting a supper club to *make* us try new places. For encouraging me to put myself first when I needed to get better. For showing me that guys can also accept your quirks. For renewing my faith in the fact that even girls who don't *need* dudes, can need a dude. And they too can accept your quirks as desirable and cute. Those who don't aren't worthy of your time. For all the bizarre memories and beautiful conversations on our epic girls' trips. You've always had my back and believed in me as I do you.

Mara—For introducing me to one of the most instrumental people in my life during this entire self-reflection period. For being an incredible light to me, an inspiration. I'm so proud of you, for having an idea and going out there and making it happen. Your loving positive energy makes the world, my world, a better place. You've been responsible for so many monumental moments of change in my life. Moments that I didn't even know would be so important and defining. I trust you implicitly.

Molly—For being the most enthusiastic advocate of all things supporting "inner beauty." For sharing your heart with me and empowering me beyond compare every single time we're together. For traveling the world with me and being a solid rock upon which I could grasp on to when I felt like I was drifting. For teaching me so many ways to believe in myself and making me feel utterly beautiful from the inside out.

Ciara—For teaching me your "girl power" ways and encouraging me to know my value, my worth. For willing what you want and being a badass mama.

The Hart family—For making Mom and me part of your family all these years. For always supporting me with whatever endeavor I do. For saving all your old photos and showing them to me just when I need to be reminded of who I am, always have been. You all mean so much to me and I'm so grateful to have you in my life.

Sheryl—For all your love and unwavering support ever since I was a wee little girl. I'm so lucky to have grown up and become your friend, no longer just the child of your friend. It's a beautiful thing when that happens. You're the most unselfish person I know and I'm a better person for knowing you.

Hilary—For the endless hours of chats over the years about anything and everything. For listening to me repeat myself time and time again, never judging, and always being there, for the good, bad, ugly, and hilarious. From the days of wearing my little white socks to those dressing up in ball gowns, it's been an adventure. You are one of a kind and I so appreciate your love, friendship, and advice.

Nick—For wanting to work with me even when I told you I didn't want to be an actress. I still can't believe I said that. But I'm so glad you said yes. For sticking by me and fighting for me every step of the way from day one. For being there as a true friend through so many trying times. For always being the best date to all our parties and for sharing in many "best nights ever." For stepping in when I didn't even know I needed you to all those years ago and for giving me hilarious but meaningful advice on men. Or boys, as you like to say. You've gone to battle for me time and time again, the ultimate knight in shining armor.

Jon—For not thinking I was crazy when I first told you I wanted to write a book but instead, introducing me to Cait and getting this whole ball rolling. For all the long sweaty hikes where you listened to me vent. For your valued opinions and determination. Thank you for believing in me and always being there as a solid friend, homie, a real bro.

Christian—For being an open ear and supportive friend.

For giving me some of the most incredible opportunities and memories I'll never forget, as well as for your straightforward, nonjudmental advice that I value and trust. Thank you for introducing me to yoga, which has calmed me down and helped introduce me to my body in new ways.

Rob and Mariel—For helping me embrace through fashion all these new sides of my personality that I never had before. You lovingly nudge me out of my comfort zone and have exposed me to so many new ways of feeling beautiful. Your artistic eyes are so inspiring and I love spending time laughing and playing with you.

Marti—For being the insancly brave woman you are. For sharing your story with me and being so honest and open from the moment I met you. Your strength and determination inspires me and being part of your film *To the Bone* played such a pivotal role in my finishing of this book. I gained such a greater understanding of myself and I'm forever grateful to you for making me feel so safe and protected. You showed me that being vulnerable is such a beautiful thing and within the most difficult of moments can come your strongest and most powerful.

Alex S.—For joining me in solidarity and giving your unwavering support during one of the most trying periods and challenging experiences of my life. For never judging me. Your heart is huge and I'm so lucky and honored to have experienced

To the Bone with you and am forever grateful having had you by my side to share these moments with. For giving me the memoir *An Apple a Day*, knowing how much it would help me during filming and beyond. Believe me, it did. You've brightened up many shadowed moments.

Christina—For keeping me sane in Korea and being my partner in crime as we explored Seoul, experiencing all the sights and sounds. I can't believe we met for the first time on that first day going to a supermarket. How totally appropriate. Little did I know how pivotal you would be in this whole recovery process during *Okja*. I don't know what I would have done without you. For encouraging me to break my no meat fast after fifteen years (even though you had no idea and felt horrible for two seconds after I told you). For being a home away from home.

Nancy—For fostering such a safe environment for me to emotionally and physically explore each and every character I portray and for all of the incredible ideas you bring to the table. Thank you for never judging my choices but instead challenging me to tap into some of the deepest parts of myself. For encouraging me to let go and be present. For the countless hours and weekend sessions you scheduled around your family time to help get me through some of the most exhausting, trying experiences and help define some of the most complex characters. I cherish our time working together and couldn't fathom having gotten through *To the Bone*, among others, without your support, love, and expertise.

Michelle—For your support over the past six years. Your light has helped me see through some of the darkest times and your insight has enabled me to reflect with a new perspective. Because of you, I've been able to accept so much of my past without shame and use what I once considered my weaknesses as my strengths. Your advice is unparalleled and your support has been invaluable. I treasure all the wisdom you've imparted to me and the positive energy you've sent my way. I don't know where I'd be without you. You've changed my life and I'm forever grateful.

Fatima—For the countless hours we've spent together in some of the most vulnerable of circumstances. Thank you for bringing such a positive vibe into my life and for always making me feel so at peace. You've taught me so much about what it feels like to be comfortable in my own skin and centered within my own body. You introduced me to a holistic philosophy that has forever changed my acknowledgment of the mind, body, and soul connection within all of us. Thank you for empowering me and making me feel like I can do anything.

Liz—For your guidance, support, and knowledge, which have taught me things I never thought I'd be open to learning. Your nonjudgmental, encouraging demeanor made all the difference in the world to my recovery period and I'll take what

I learned in our sessions with me forever. I'm so thankful the universe made us meet when we did.

Cait—For believing in me and my story and making all of this become a reality. I couldn't have done this without your guidance and passion.

Sara—For being my incredible editor, without whom none of this would have happened. For never judging my story but, instead, embracing it as if it were your own and being the most amazing sounding board upon which I bounced countless ideas at all hours of the day. Thank you for always answering my questions, no matter how big or small, so unbelievably fast, and for letting me use your awesome office when you were away. I felt so legit. Thank you for never pressuring me and always making sure I felt comfortable and safe. For all the laughs and hours of editing over rushed lunches and countless cups of tea. For never filtering my voice. For never questioning my intentions and making sure I felt safe and protected and yet creatively challenged. For understanding me from the second we met. Even though *this* book is all finished, our friendship remains. I'm so so happy the universe brought us together. Everything really does happen for a reason.

The rest of my amazing team at HarperCollins—For your incredible passion and belief in me from the get-go. Thank you to Veronica Ambrose, Bess Braswell, Barbara Fitzsimmons,

Alison Donalty, Cindy Hamilton, Stephanie Hoover, Kate Jackson, Alison Klapthor, Jennifer Klonsky, Ro Romanello, Nellie Kurtzman, the entire Sales team, Suzanne Murphy, Anna Prendella, Emily Rader, and Elizabeth Ward for encouraging my ideas, embracing my story, and protecting my voice. You so graciously welcomed me in as part of the family and showed me the ropes when I invaded Sara's office. Working alongside all of you during that last week of finishing everything up was an experience I'll never ever forget. It made this whole journey extra-special and perfectly complete. You made going to work every day so fun and fulfilling. I couldn't have done this without all of your hard work, collaboration, and dedication. We did it!

Dean—For all your help over the years and for always making me laugh just when I needed to. Thank you for all the random conversations during our fun airport car rides. For never judging my outfit choices (God knows you've witnessed some of my questionable phases), but for also never being shy about telling me your honest opinions. They're pretty much all on point. I so appreciate all you've done for Mom and me, and I value our friendship.

Ella—For being the beautiful, sweet, smart, magnetic young woman that you are. Thank you for teaching me so much about myself even when you had no idea you were. Your poise and elegance, wit and charm inspire me and I'm so proud of you.

Never forget who you are and never, ever settle for anything or anyone less than you deserve. I know your parents wouldn't let that happen but I'm going to keep telling you regardless. You're an incredibly special human being and I'm lucky to know you.

Lancôme—For encouraging women of all ages around the world to embrace our inner beauty and accept ourselves as we are. For enhancing our already unique personalities, instilling inner confidence, and brightening our inner glow. Thank you for recognizing our differences as unique, defining characteristics, not flaws. For your loyalty and belief in me. It's a privilege to represent the brand alongside such strong, talented, and inspiring women and an absolute honor to be part of the family.

All of the other brave young souls who have shared their stories with me on social media and in person—For inspiring me every single day with your words and support. The love you show not only me but one another is utterly beautiful. I never expected to be part of such an incredibly encouraging community of young men and women as the one that I have on social media. Thank you for your stunning handmade books and gifts. For your messages and well wishes. For making me smile when I needed to most. For fostering a safe environment in which to share and connect. Your bravery to put yourselves out there, openness and willingness to speak your minds, and strength to bare your innermost thoughts inspired me to do the same. Truly. Thank you from the bottom of my heart for your daily messages, photos, and drawings. They have provided me more comfort than you'll ever know. Your passion and dedication is unparalleled and I'm honored to know you all.

RESOURCES

While all efforts have been made to ensure the accuracy of the information in the following sections as of the date this book was published, it is for informational purposes only. It is not intended to be complete or exhaustive, or a substitute for the advice of a qualified expert or mental health professional.

If there's anything I talked about that you or someone you know could relate to and wanted to learn more about, here are some specific resources. Remember, asking for help and seeking support is never a sign of weakness. It takes strength and bravery. Whatever it is you're struggling with, you don't have to go through it alone.

EATING DISORDER RESOURCES

* Bulimia.com: bulimia.com

* Center for Eating Disorders: center4ed.org/resources.
  asp

* Eating Disorder Hope: eatingdisorderhope.com

* Eating Disorder Referral and Information Center:
  edreferral.com

* The Healthy Teen Project: healthyteenproject.com

* National Eating Disorders Association:
  nationaleatingdisorders.org

Along with the novel *Eat Cake* by Jeanne Ray, the memoir *An Apple a Day* by Emma Woolf was an incredible source of inspiration for me while I was on my path to recovery in Seoul after *To the Bone* and while finishing this book. Emma's bravery in exposing her disordered history, her writing's blunt delivery and brutal honesty, and the way she holds herself accountable for her actions in order to move forward encouraged me to dig deeper within my own struggles and be more honest with myself. To write more openly. To let go and live more freely.

DATING ABUSE RESOURCES

* Break the Cycle: breakthecycle.org

* loveisrespect: loveisrespect.org

* The National Domestic Violence Hotline: thehotline. org

BULLYING RESOURCES

* The Bully Project: thebullyproject.com

* Bystander Revolution: bystanderrevolution.org

* Olweus Bullying Prevention Program: violencepreventionworks.org

* PACER's National Bullying Prevention Center: pacer. org/bullying

* Stop Bullying: stopbullying.gov

* Teen Line: teenlineonline.org

* The WE Movement: we.org

GENERAL MENTAL HEALTH RESOURCES

* Crisis Text Line: crisistextline.org

* It Gets Better Project: itgetsbetter.org

* National Alliance on Mental Illness: nami.org

* The Trevor Project: thetrevorproject.org

ABOUT THE AUTHOR

Entertainment has been a big part of Lily Collins's life since her childhood in England. Once she moved to Los Angeles, Lily attended the Youth Academy of Dramatic Arts and performed in numerous musical theater productions. In 2009, Lily made her film debut in the Academy Award–nominated film *The Blind Side*, and in 2016, she was nominated for a Golden Globe for Best Actress in a Motion Picture Comedy or Musical for her performance in Warren Beatty's *Rules Don't Apply*. Her other projects include the films *Priest*; *Abduction*; *Mirror Mirror*; *The English Teacher*; *Stuck in Love*; *The Mortal Instruments*: *City of Bones*; *Love, Rosie*; *To the Bone*; *Okja*; and *Halo of Stars*, as well as the TV series *The Last Tycoon*. Lily also has a passion for journalism, which she discovered at the age of fifteen while working for *ELLE Girl* UK. Later, she reported on the 2008 presidential election for Nickelodeon, covered the Democratic and Republican National Conventions in a *Seventeen* magazine blog, and was a contributing editor for *CosmoGirl* and the *Los Angeles Times Magazine*. Lily has always strived to empower young people to use their voices, starting in high school, where she trained to be a teen therapist. Within the last few years, she has taken part in national events focused on encouraging today's youth to stand together and speak out. This is Lily's debut book.